The survival of an organization: Technology + Cyber

Jeffrey Lush –
Jeffrey.l.lush@gmail.com

First Printing: January 2019

ISBN: 978-0-359-36535-7

Purchase printed book, or other titles at: http://www.lulu.com or Amazon.com. Search for Jeffrey Lush.

Contents

Introduction

The survival of an organization is impacted by the technology and cybersecurity strategies deployed within the organization, the decisions we have or are getting ready to make. As individuals, we make decisions based on multiple indicators or events, applying an unspoken weight or priority to arrive at a conclusion. For example, while driving your car you notice that the temperature of your vehicle is increasing, the air conditioner is now delivering warmer air, and you smell an almost sweet odor coming from your vents. Within minutes, you see steam coming from the hood of the vehicle. All these events put together definitely indicate that your car is about to overheat. As a result of these isolated events occurring, you know that engine failure is imminent if you do not turn off the car. We make decisions, in this example to turn off the vehicle (increased vehicle temperature, smell, and steam) every day. There are many indicators within our technology and cyber environments that can help us define if failure is imminent, decisions that we make often. Are we making the correct technology and cyber choices?

picture 1 – radiator overheating

The content of this book focuses on the many decisions we make as organization leaders that unavoidably have connections to technology and cyber practices. We will explore technology and cyber-based solutions to common organizational challenges that have a direct impact on profitability and efficiencies. We will review:

- cloud vs. local technologies
- sharing of data
- task management
- video conferencing

Technology Availability

As of December 2018, organizations have many alternatives when designing technologies that will be used to satisfy business needs. The content of this book discusses several approaches to evaluating the need to optimize cost related to information technology.

Shortly following the devastating terrorist attacks in the United States, many large organizations became keenly aware of their need to replicate data (see technical details "Building a Persistent Computing Environment" within this book) in the remote chance of another terrorist attack. The following example is from one of the world's largest legal organizations.

Scenario: The legal organization has office throughout the globe, although most of their data resided in the Eastern United States. The legal organization was committed to near losing any data, an admirable objective. They have three primary data centers within 500 miles of one another. They were convinced that synchronous replication between sites or zero data loss must exist and that the performance they currently experience at each of the three primary sites should remain unaffected.

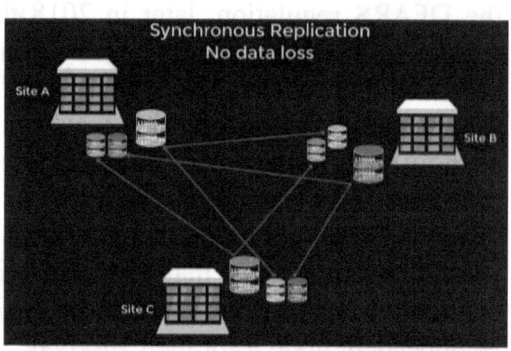

figure 1 - Synchronous Replication

Architecture for the Scenario: we proposed a synchronous replication architecture as that was the only type of architecture that would guarantee zero data loss between the three sites. To achieve the same level of performance, high-speed, very expensive network connectivity was required between all three locations.

This is one example of the availability of technology coupled with the reality of cost. The key to success is not to understand some of the parts of the puzzle, but to have a comprehensive vision of all pieces of the puzzle. With a broad understanding of available technology and a disciplined evaluation process of solutions built upon functionality, performance, manageability, and fiscal accountability the proper technology was deployed to meet the customer's expectations and budget. The contents of this book will strengthen your discipline and knowledge in making the right technology and cyber decisions within your organization.

Conclusion of scenario: the final design for this customer was a mixture of synchronous and asynchronous technologies discussed in greater detail within this book in the *"Building a Persistent Computing Environment"* section.

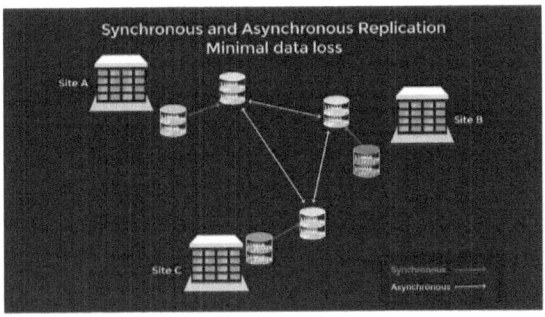

figure 2 - Asynchronous Replication

 4- minute video discussing synchronous and asynchronous replication example: https://youtu.be/a9JjnWqYP4s

Understanding the technology, we use within our organization is a critical variable in the decision process for all stakeholders. The content herein is designed to provide some data points and essential questions to make the decisions needed for your organization. The cost and cyber risk to an organization can be devastating if the choices are not founded in knowledge and experience.

Embracing change

There are many variables when evaluating the effectiveness of change in our environment, and herein we will explore the decision variables as it relates to technology enablement and accountability for remote employees.

I grew up in a small town in California called Green Valley Lake (GVL). GVL was a beautiful place to grow up, with less than 100 full-time residents, a lake for the summer and a ski hill for the winter. It was common practice to leave your keys in the ignition of your car or above the sun visor, and our homes were unlocked most of the time. When I think of existing infrastructure in most organizations, I think of GVL. Existing infrastructure that was built from the ground up for over 30 years, and in most cases, very trusting of the users within the environment.

A few years later while serving in the military, I lived in the Republic of XYZ. In XYZ it was commonplace to build large cinder block walls around your homes, cement broken glass on top of the walls and place iron shutters on your windows. I liken the Republic of XYZ to the development of Cloud technology. Developers understood that Cloud services would be open to the world, and security would be critical to success, just as citizens of the Republic of XYZ knew their safety was partially dependent on cinder block walls topped with sharp glass pieces.

The example is important as we make decisions for our organizations. Too often organizations make decisions under pretense, that their local infrastructure is more secure than a cloud infrastructure. Based on my experience, many organizations would increase their security posture by using cloud services. These are all decision points that only the organization can answer. Let's focus on two primary variables in this decision-making process related to remote employees:

Enabling Software as a Service

How can an organization efficiently and cost-effectively provide remote employees with the tools needed to complete their tasks without threatening the security of the organization? These type of services, frequently called "Software as a Service (SaaS)" can be leveraged to support internal and remote employees.

Software as a Service provides access to applications that can be used through a web browser. These types of services are wonderful for organizations and individuals that would like the services provided to large organizations, without having the knowledge, time, or resources to set up the services within their small business or homes.

Online services include almost anything that you would like to get done online. Listed below you can find some popular services with brief definitions of the service. Review the list for possible integration points into your environment. This is not a complete list, as there are hundreds of thousands of services available online.

Managing Systems

Challenge: Updating user machines is a challenge, especially remote employees' machines. Many organizations are shifting from organization provided equipment to employee provide equipment. Typically, the organization provides an annual allowance and employees are expected to maintain their equipment. With over 1 billion subscribers to office 365, moving an organization to a cloud-based office automation solution is a quick win. Office automation applications include word processing, spreadsheet functionality, development of presentations, email, calendaring, shared files and collaboration.

- The most popular of the services are either Microsoft Office 365 Google Docs / Suite. Both services provide email, spreadsheets, presentations and documents that can be created, managed and shared with others. Both services come with "off-line" capabilities and for the most part are compatible with one another.
- Many services offer a free online experience, although with Microsoft Office 365 the free experience is very limited, whereas the free experience with Google is much more robust. From an application perspective though, Microsoft Office 365 is very close to their office automation suite, offering the most powerful office automation suite in the market. Google Docs, although a great service as well, is not as commonly used for business applications as is Microsoft office 365. You will need to decide as to what works best for your environment. Some key points to consider:
- How many email addresses do you require? And how much is a new email address? Do you require the email address to have your domain name, for example, @sears.com or is a random domain name acceptable, for example, @msn.com or @gmail.com.
  - Will you always be using the tools online, or will you require off-line access? Off-line access means that you can continue to use the functionality of the application while you are not connected to the Internet, for example, while flying in an airplane with no Internet capabilities.
  - Do you require services outside of email, documents, spreadsheets, and presentations? If the answer is yes, you may want to consider a software provider that integrates all those functions.

Secure Data

Challenge: Organization information cannot be secured properly with remote employees. The security of an organizations data is critical, and except for highly sensitive information shared in defense of our nation, all other data can be protected with the correct technology in place.

- Organizations can leverage several data loss prevention (DLP) solutions. A DLP solution will allow the organization the ability to set limits on files and folders, for example, when and where the file can be opened, expire the file, or remove all data from the file. Microsoft Office 365 also has DLP functionality throughout the suite of offerings.
- Software-based encryption. Popular tools include AXCrypy, BestCrypt, and others.
- Hardware-based encryption. Popular tools include self-encrypting hard drives, Microsoft BitLocker and others.
- The protection of data is important for remote and internal users. In most cases, the same technology used internally can be used for remote employees.

Staying in Touch

Challenge: Employees must be together to collaborate on projects and be inspired by one another. Multiple technologies enable collaboration without the need to be in the same building. Some organizations must be within the same physical location due to security requirements, for example, employees that are dealing with top secret information are typically grouped into a single location. The services business cannot support remote workers, at least for many of the jobs as they are serving others, for example, restaurants, hotels, and entertainment. Although, for several employees, remote work is very possible. Three primary concerns include:

- A lack of understanding related to the solutions currently enabling remote workers.
- Low bandwidth at remote employee locations.
- Accountability of the employee, are they working or playing at home?

Let's go ahead and address each of the concerns with available technology.

Technology that enables remote workers

Remote workers, just like corporate workers require specific tools to complete their duties:

- **Desktop PC or Laptop**: In many environments, the desktop, laptop, tablet (known as a workstation) are provided by the individual employee. An allowance is often provided for the employee with the understanding that the employee is responsible for completing their work, maintaining the computer and arranging for service if the workstation fails. From a business perspective, the burden of workstation management and refresh cycles is a considerable cost, besides, the remote employee reduces the cost of the hardware, software and support staff for the business. Some organizations provide a desktop to the remote employee as well.

- **Encryption**: Encryption is designed to protect digital assets and is no different for a remote worker. The US Federal Government has a standard called FIPS 140-2. Within FIPS 140-2 data at rest and data in flight are encrypted and monitored. Encryption of data is closely related to a "Data Loss Prevention (DLP)" functionality.

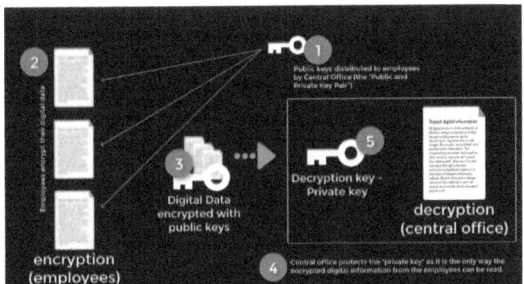

figure 4 - Asymmetric Encryption

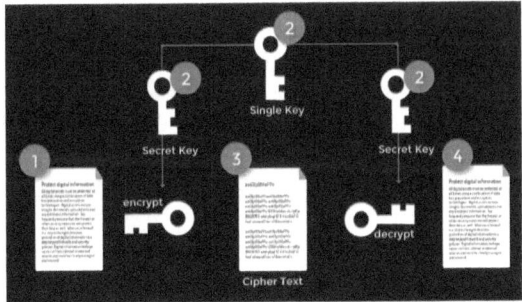

figure 3 - Symmetric Encryption

Encryption essentially wraps the digital asset with digital protection that is only unlocked with the correct "key." There are multiple types of encryption to include: Asymmetric and Symmetric. Asymmetric encryption uses a public and private key pair (as illustrated), whereas Symmetric encryption consists of one key for encryption and decryption.

- **Internet Access** can be a challenge for remote employees. Although many of the technologies today support processes that allow the remote desktop to synchronize data with the server as bandwidth is available. Internet access must support conference and video calls, although many key technologies like Zoom and Skype have done a great job managing calls with limited bandwidth.

- **Phone services** can be satisfied using cellular plans, Internet-based phone, video/phone conferencing or public PBX services like RingCentral. Dependent on the size of your organization, one of the technologies will meet your needs. Many small businesses use an Internet-based PBX (Private branch exchange – phone system) that allows them to work throughout the globe, although customers calling into the "office" have the same experience of a "bricks and mortar office."

- **Virtual Private Network** is the ability to extend your current "internal" network with validated external access.

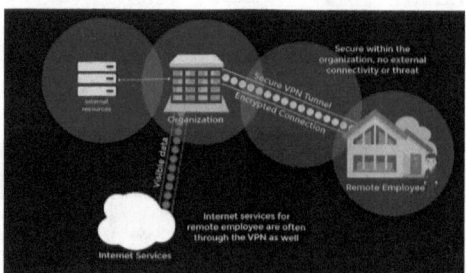

Remote employees can create an extension of your network to their remote location, with all the associated security controls. VPN access is typically provided to access

figure 5 - VPN

applications and services that have not or are unable to migrate to a cloud service, for example, an internal financial system or manufacturing system.

 1min video on VPN: https://goo.gl/jnEKCD

- **Image / Video** design for organizations that need to stretch beyond standard PowerPoint. There are several services available online. Interested in creating infomercials (video and messaging?), it is easy with Biteable. For more detailed work checkout Camtasia and/or the Adobe Suite. If you are using Windows10, you may want to check out Grapholite. Years ago, I would have suggested Microsoft Visio, although for many users the mentioned suites are simple to use and get the job done. For drawing checkout SketchBook Pro, certainly if you are using a tablet.

1min video on Asymmetric Encryption: https://goo.gl/D5AGzM
2min video on Symmetric Encryption: https://goo.gl/Eyg9qW

- **Video Conferencing** is a large market with multiple solutions available. Microsoft Skype is very popular, although it can be a little inconsistent at times. Zoom is a nice alternative to Skype, although there are thousands of applications for video conferencing. Be clear on your expectation for the video conferencing platform and search for value. Many video conferencing platforms allow for a "free trial." Check out the platforms for your environment, and to create a worst-case scenario, before testing the video conferencing, begin a large download or upload or processor/memory heavy application to see how well the platform performs with other tasks.
- **Financial** software ranges from tools like Xero to Intuit and many others. Several financial packages provide software as a service, which may warrant a closer review.

Enabling Accountability for workloads

The evaluation of remote employees from a technology perspective must be centered in a defined business evaluation process. The *"Aligning Technology and Business"* section of this book provides details on making technology decisions. **Accountability**: how do we maintain accountability of remote employees? How can we ensure that the job is getting done, regardless of their work location?

Many organizations believe that remote employees add a different level of risk to the organization, let's look at a few of the common concerns:

- **Task Management** is directly tied to accountability for all employees, remote or local. Many organizational leaders meet more considerable expectations like a revenue goal, or employee retention, although struggle with establishing tasks and objectives for themselves or their employees. Accountability for employee productivity for some organizations can be measured by the number of widgets produced or the amount of revenue obtained, although the absence of task management cripples' and organization from reaching their full potential. Task management starts at the top of the organization, and filters into the employees with defined expectations on a daily, weekly or monthly basis. Measuring and tracking expectations is simple in today's world of software tools like Asana and others.

Enabling remote employees must be reviewed by the organization and their specific needs, although I would submit that there are significant benefits from enabling a remote workforce, which include:

- **Happier employees**. The rigors of traffic and congested buildings wear on the employee's moral. Better work to life balance. The employee oversees their schedule, not held at the office, even though the work is done.
- **Increased productivity**. Many remote employees work harder and more extended total hours than other employees. Contrary to the myth, remote employees are not at home watching TV and eating Bonbons.
- **Better solutions and products**. Creativity is easily expressed within the confines of a space that is free from interruption and focused on job expectations.
- **Increased collaboration**. As video conferencing is the norm, collaboration with multiple employees does not require a conference room and connecting the projector, employees simple share their screens in video conferencing.

All employees require direction and clearly stated objectives. As organizations embrace task management and employee accountability, the location of the employee should be the least concern.

QRT – Understanding your needs	
Summary of Understanding your needs	Many technologies are discussed in this section of the book. The key to understanding your needs is to be open to the possibility of change. Too often we are shackled by our memories of yesteryear, that we fail to see the cost benefit to changing our technology and cyber needs.
Complexity of implementation	The implementation of many of the technologies discussed within this section is straightforward to deploy many environments are already using the tools, although they may need to extend their functionality.
Starting fresh	If you are starting from scratch, and are a small organization, look at the services provided by the cloud. Several products are discussed herein. If you are a larger organization, evaluation of your existing technology investments balanced with a definite "objective" plan will allow you to discover the gaps in your strategy, as well introduce new technologies.
Modifying existing environment	For existing environments, in most cases, identifying and validating current software is the first step. Identify software based on functionality that is discovered through reading this section. This is not about identifying names of products, as the implementation of the product will vary considerably. Identify the "function" the software is currently providing to the organization.
Business Interruption	Minimal business interruption should occur.
Ballpark Pricing	There will be pricing associated with the identification of software assets and their functionality. Service cost for many of the solutions run from $50.00 per month per user to $150.00 per month per user. The key is to have a well-

	defined functionality chart and only purchase the services and quantities you need.
Learning Curve	There is a minimal learning curve.
FTE or Contractor	The collection of inventories does not require a lot of decisions throughout the process, making this an activity for anyone with the desire to work. Once inventory has been collected, a different skill set may be required to organize the inventory into systems based on your operational needs.
Hints to get started	Start with defining your desired objectives. Review the section and document how you will leverage the technology to build a stronger organization. The goals are a critical step, as all decisions will go back to the objectives. Understand the software that is active in your environment today. You may be surprised that you have all the technology you need to get started.
Videos	- 1-minute video on VPN: https://goo.gl/jnEKC - 1- minute video on Asymmetric Encryption: https://goo.gl/D5AGzM - 2-minute video on Symmetric Encryption: https://goo.gl/Eyg9qW - 4-minute video discussing synchronous and asynchronous replication example: https://youtu.be/a9JjnWqYP4s

Chapter 2: Aligning Technology and Business

How will I arrive, if I never know where I am going?

As we focus our effort, attention, and passion on identifying a destination, clarity is within view, and we arrive. Defining the technology destination is critical to the success of any organization. The destination we seek is the ability to serve the recipient of the technology and to create an environment that technology works for the organization, not the organization working for the technology. Explore with me some of the "mile markers" along the road to our destination.

Mile Marker 1 : Basics of technology

Before we begin on this journey to define a technology and organizations destination, we should have a baseline of understanding for our journey:

- **Client access**: client access is the ability the client has access information within the technology environment. The user may be using a desktop, laptop or mobile device. Access to the information and technology resources may be "inside" the organization, or connection may be required from a remote location. Whatever the circumstance, client access should be available anytime, anywhere.
    - **Usernames and passwords are external to my environment**. Management of usernames and passwords can be accomplished exactly
- **Servers**: servers host the "services" that are presented to the client. Servers are very similar to desktops, with the exception the server has additional resources that will support hundreds, even thousands of users.
- **Storage**: storage is used in support of the desktop and the server. Typically, storage will either host performance, short-term and or long-term storage needs.
- **Networks**: many "networks" can be found within an organization. In ethernet network historically provides connectivity from the desktop to the server, and connectivity from the server to the storage. Within high-performance environments, Ethernet connects the desktops

to the servers and, the servers connect to the storage area network using a fibre channel network. Fibre channel network support high-speed transactions on a network. Many network support enterprise infrastructures.

- **Security:** security is the ability to secure all data and access to the processing power that resides on the desktop, storage, servers, and networks. Security is designed to protect the integrity of the information stored within the organization from unauthorized access within an external to the organization.

- **Persistent computing architecture**: working within many parameters set by security, a persistent computing architecture provides consistent access to services and resources within the organization. Persistent computing architecture provides availability and recoverability of data and services on the desktop, server, storage, and network.

- **Services**: services are the functionality provided to the users of the technology. For example: when an email is read, the email services provide the information and data requested.

Mile Marker 2: Customer is always first

As we proceed to mile marker to, we understand some of the basics of enterprise architecture. It makes sense; the user requests a service, the network delivers the request to a server and or storage, the server and storage provide the required service/information to the user. The key to success in this model is the consistency of the service provided. Service consistency can be broken into two primary objectives: availability and performance.

- **Availability**: persistence and the availability of the service. Is my email always available?

- **Performance**: the application will perform well, all the time, every time. Can I get access to my email?

Mile Marker 3: Accountable customer experience

As we continue our journey, it is important to understand potential road closures, construction, and possible weather conditions may impede our progress. We collect the information through access to multiple "collection agents" along the way. Within an enterprise architecture, we collect "intelligence" (information) from various data points and sources along the way. The collection of the information compiled and understood can be a great benefit to all travelers. The absence of this information is almost guaranteed to produce a negative experience for the traveler. We must be able to collect the necessary information to make decisions.

Mile Marker 4: Making a decision

Success related to enterprise architecture is the ability to gain consensus among all users of the technology. The process must have the ability to solicit and evaluate input consistently. The most expeditious manner of arriving at the destination is to plot a course allowing others to modify the course based on experience and best practices. Planning a trip without a destination on your mind only exasperates the challenge of arriving at the desired destination.

Building a structure that is scalable, consistent, and fair for the evaluation of all technology and business-impacting decisions is critical to success. Mile Marker 5 will review the concept of four primary decision criteria and weighted values.

Mile Marker 5: Decision criteria

There are four primary decision criteria to consider when evaluating technology. The four primary decision criteria include:

- **Functionality**: what is the desired feature(s) of the solution? What does the end-user need to perform their business objectives?
- **Performance**: what are the performance expectations from the services delivered? What is the justification for the performance required? Can the performance be evaluated consistently and in a repeatable manner?
- **Manageability:** what are the manageability features within the solution and do they align with the needs of the organization? Does the organization have the correct skill set to manage new features and solutions?
- **Fiscal Accountability:** is there similar technology within the organization that can be leveraged or expanded? Can some expectations of the technology be adjusted to reduce or avoid the expenditure?

To evaluate a solution, you must have the ability to review all facets of the solution and use a weighted scale to make a business decision. Review the four primary decision criteria listed above or create your own and consistently evaluate technology based upon your organization's needs.

Technology is not about products or vendors; it is about functionality to perform a specific service required by the business. The weighted decision criteria will allow for the business to make decisions related to the technology as it meets business needs. For example, the solution presented requires an operating system (X) which costs $100,000 with annual maintenance of $30,000. An alternative operating system (Y) is available at $20,000 with yearly maintenance of $2000. The solution is evaluated based upon the four primary decision criteria. The evaluation looks something like the following:

- requirement: 1000 I/O's per second (IOPS)
- operating system (X) performs at 1000 IOPS
- operating system (Y) performs at 900 IOPS

The decision criteria that are impacted by this example are performance and fiscal accountability. To get an accurate picture of the decision criteria and a weighted analysis, let's look at a few of the numbers. Technically the solution will perform on both operating systems (X) and (Y).

	Purchase Cost	Labor	Annual Maintenance (30%)	5-year cost for maintenance	Total Investment
Operating System (X)	$100,000	$100,000	$30,000	$150,000	$350,000
Operating System (Y)	$20,000	$20,000	$6,000	$30,000	$70,000
				Cost for 100 IOPs	$280,000

The business question: what is the business justification to pay $280,000 over the next five years for 100 IOPS?

Some examples of questions used to support the four primary decision criteria:

Functionality:
- In the event of a failure, how will we recover the service and data?
- Where is the backup data being written?
- How large is the data requirement?
- What is the mixture of performance computing and storage versus standard performance and storage?

Performance:
- Will data be replicated within the data center or to another data center?
- What are the performance objectives for the server, storage, and network?
- What are the dependencies in recovery order in the event of a failure?

Manageability:
- What technology is in place to ensure rapid recovery of the solution?
- What technology is in place to provide stability of the service within the environment?
- Is there sensitive data within the environment? If so how is that data being identified?

Fiscal Accountability:
- Can an existing investment be leveraged?
- What is the operating system?

Mile Marker 6: Communication

Developing a core infrastructure to support the amount of information required for a technical analysis review is tied closely to the success of the process. The communication needs to be simple, easy to access, and capable of supporting multiple projects and solutions working in parallel. The communication model must scale as a requirement within the process scales.

With the continued popularity of Internet browsers, the first step is to develop portals for information gathering and dissemination. Portals can be as simple as a managed, centralized access point for all information to a complex desktop application that synchronizes information on a regular basis.

Why not use email to provide information? Email, in general, is less than efficient when collecting multiple data points. Email does not allow for proper accountability or historical information often required to make informed decisions. The integration of email into a shared data portal can be a workable solution.

Email is overwhelming; hence the need to deliver a consistent "look and feel" to all email traffic associated with the process is the key to success. Using the same key phrase in the subject line, the same image in the email body can easily allow users to identify relevant information quickly. Some examples to use within email include:

- Create a visual association with a logo or colors and specific fonts.
- The email header always contains the same type of information, for example, a project name and the desired outcome in a repeatable format.
- Consistency within the message body header. For example, include the project name, the action item, the estimated time required to complete the task, and the suspense or due date of the task.

Mile Marker 7: Technology review

Making significant progress in the journey to our destination. We successfully understood the importance of lexicon in our priorities in mile marker one, two and three. We have reviewed the requirement and the strength of using a weighted decision matrix at mile marker for a mile marker five and discussed some communication ideas and mile marker number six.

Before we proceed with our journey, let's discuss how to conduct a technology review the information we've collected. The technology review is designed to expose new technologies. Technology analysis review provides the following information:

- **Basics and standards**: reviewed the general concepts of the proposed technology and established some initial standards.
- **Business value**: associate the solution with business values designed to build efficiencies and lower operating costs.

Preparing for the road trip

Developing enterprise architectures like taking a road trip. We start with the needed supplies: enthusiastic passengers, a roadmap, car keys, inflated tires preventive maintenance on the vehicle, all important if you plan to arrive at your destination. Also, enterprise architecture requires several key "supplies" to be successful:

- Business requirements of capture to find the needs of the business.
- Technology review to merge the captured business need with the technology.

At Mile Marker 4 and 5 we discussed the value of making informed decisions, and our first road trip supply will be a review of the architecture decision matrix.

Architecture decision matrix

Technology prioritization is important to the balance of workload throughout any organization. The architecture decision matrix leverages a weighting system that evaluates a solution to multiple criteria. The concept is to evaluate the technology as logically as possible. Multiple weighted questions assist the evaluator in exploring the actual value of the decision while masking the results until all questions of been answered. The concept behind the architecture decision matrix is to establish an unbiased selection of technology.

- Step 1: clearly define the business objectives or the functional outcome desired by the business.
- Step 2: now that the business objectives are identified, develop questions that support the objectives.
- Step 3: build the evaluation criteria. Evaluation criteria allow for the participant to "rate" the value of the decision variable (the question) as an alliance to the objective.
- Step 4: enroll others in the decision-making process. The decision-making process allows multiple people to review the business objectives, provide answers and feedback to the questions submitted. Feedback received will produce a better decision and solution.

The output of the architecture decision matrix includes:

- **Weighted evaluation** of submitted answers correlating the proposed technology to the business objectives. A review committee provides scores based upon the responses received. Remember the aim is to align the solution to the defined business objectives.
- **Financial evaluation** provides estimates on cost, labor and reoccurring cost.

Please see additional books on the architecture decision matrix (ADM) for details.

Standards

A list of items to include for the road trip, or a standard configuration of items (a tire ranch, a jack, flares, etc.) Are critical to our safety and success.

The picture below is representative of many information technology infrastructures. The walls of the infrastructure are different technologies that only address an immediate need. Windows and doors are missing due to the absence of vision coupled with minimal compliance with standards. The house may keep the elements out, although susceptible to failure and elevated risk producing an inconsistent

picture 2 – limited standards-based infrastructure

customer experience, data loss, poor performance, inadequate security, and an increased cost burden.

Developing standards is a critical first step to establishing a sound enterprise infrastructure. Standards for building functional requirements and not vendor preferences. Enterprise infrastructure that is designed for flexibility and compliance with functional requirements will always provide cost efficiencies and performance enhancements. Functional compliance will break the "vendor architecture" that too often runs prevalent within organizations and frequently thwarts the introduction of emerging technologies. The business should always dictate the need and allow the technology to satisfy the demand. Establishing and sustaining standards is key to enabling functional requirements which will unavoidably reduce cost related to information technology.

Understanding and establishing standards is the first step. The standards must have an action related to them, or they will be useless in the environment. The standard should outline with great detail the functional requirements for acquisition activities. For example: when specifying hard disk types for storage and server environments, the performance related to the hard drive should be the driving functional requirement and the evaluation criteria for acquisition. Organizations should avoid specifying specific vendors or industry hard drive types like SAS or Fiber. Present the functional requirement, the performance required for that hard disk to meet business needs, and allow vendors to satisfy the requirement. You will be amazed at the creativity and innovations you will invite into your environment that will ultimately increase your performance and reduce your cost.

When we build an enterprise infrastructure with a set of plans and a consistent approach the results will include an accountable customer

experience and enhanced security and cost savings. With the application of standards to our enterprise infrastructure we will drive down cost and increase efficiencies. The image below represents a technology infrastructure that is built upon standards.

picture 3 - standards based infrastructure

Evaluating the solution

Now that we have collected the information, we will need to perform an evaluation before moving to an acquisition. While on our road trip, we will unavoidably encounter challenges along the way, although we have appropriately prepared our ability to mitigate risk and resolve problems is greatly enhanced.

The technical analysis review process is a process flow designed to consistently validate all technical solutions against the four primary analysis criteria for information technology implementations. Each of the four fundamental analysis criteria receives a weighted score to the evaluation process as discussed in previous sections. Your weights may vary depending upon your business objectives.

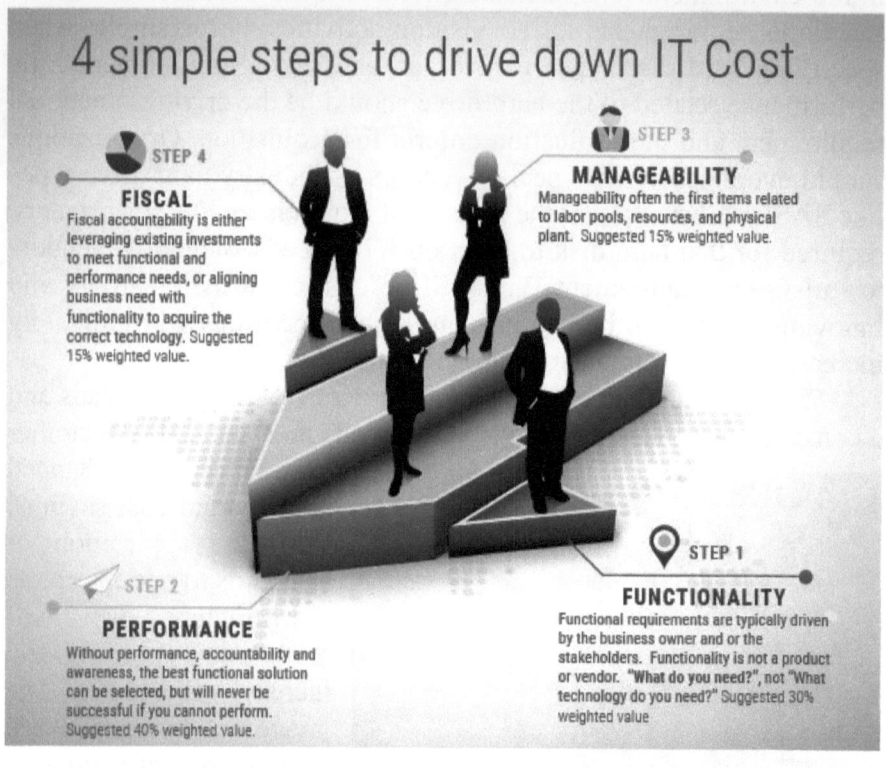

picture 4 - drive down IT cost

Functionality: the functionality of a solution is critical to the success of any organization. Functional requirements are typically driven by the business owner and or the stakeholders. The speed at which a file is retrieved within the infrastructure, or the record processed, are examples of functional requirements. The weighted value for functionality typically is 30% of the final decision.

Performance: the performance of a solution allows the functionality of the solution to be successful. Without performance accountability and awareness, the best functional solution can be selected, but will never be successful if you cannot perform. The weighted for performance typically represents 40% of the final decision.

Manageability: the ability to manage the solution is very important for the success of both functionality and performance. Manageability often the first items related to labor pools, resources, and physical plant. The weighted value for manageability typically represents 15% of the final decision.

Fiscally responsible: fiscal accountability and responsibility is often the result of leveraging existing investments and future infrastructure to optimize reoccurring maintenance costs and minimize capital investment. The weighted value for fiscal responsibility represents 15% of the final decision.

The weighted values are variables that can be adjusted based on business requirements and should be discussed with all interested parties. Once a weighted value has been established for the organization they should be applied equally to all technology decisions.

Now that we understand the primary analysis criteria on which the technical analysis is conducted, let's review some of the common questions associated with each analysis criteria. An understanding of the questions will assist all interested parties in developing solutions that are complete. Some of the questions are listed below, although it is important to realize that not all questions can be summarized within this document as often are very dependent upon the solution being reviewed.

Functionality: questions are focused on the functionality of the application and solution.
- What type of front-end servers will be required? If any?
- If the operating system is not an organization standard, questions related to the performance requirements and functionality of the alternative operating system should be asked.
- If the solution appears to have excessive hardware requirements, justifications and issues surrounding those requirements should be asked.
- A drawing defining the roles of the servers, storage, infrastructure and applications should be a requirement and part of the review process.

Performance: questions are focused on the performance of the application and solution:

- What are the performance requirements and service-level agreements/customer expectations for the application/solution?
- If the solution is storing data, questions around the data warehouse, backup and recovery, high-availability and rapid recovery should be part of the review process.
- Questions focused on the availability of services. Availability of services will be directly related to the business requirements and expectations set by the business owner. A common question asked, "how long can you be without this service?"
- What is the performance requirement of the network? A question should focus on local area network needs, wireless network needs, and wide area network requirements.
- How are data and services replicated? A common question asked? "How much data can you lose and how long can you be without a specific service and data?

Manageability: questions are focused on the manageability of the solution within the current environment.
- Can the application/solution be adapted to a virtualized environment?
- Does the solution operating system differ from the organization standard operating system?
- Questions around the physical plant and requirements related to power and network bandwidth requirements.

Fiscal Accountability: questions are focused on the financial accountability of the solution:
- Can an existing investment be leveraged to host the solution?
- Can the solution be integrated into a current procurement to create economies of scale?

Leveraging current investments

All organizations produce a degree of technology fragmentation. For example: in excess of 150 tool to manage the network have been identified within the organization. Leveraging the existing investment will assist in standards, although almost always provide cost savings.

The evaluation process reviews standards and integration into an enterprise infrastructure. Effective management of a large enterprise must be built on standards and monitored for proactive service levels through the aggregation of intelligence agents and monitors position throughout the enterprise.

The reduction of redundant tools becomes clear as functional requirements and standards are implemented throughout the environment. This allows organizations to reduce current operating expense and increase efficiencies throughout the organization. Redundant tools and applications within the organization not only create a financial burden but present a substantial security risk to the environment.

Producing results

Developing standards and evaluation processes as defined on the previous pages is difficult, although producing results from your effort is a considerable undertaking as the concepts may push against existing processes and culture.

Path of least resistance

All solutions should be evaluated upon the four primary evaluation criteria (functionality, performance, manageability and fiscal accountability). Based on resources, all solution may not require the same amount of time to complete the technical review process, although imperative, all solution should endure the same level of rigor.

Many of us are anxious to be accommodating and to please others and may be tempted to "fast-track" the solution ignoring the technology review process discussed herein. Although "fast-tracking" produces immediate results, the results more frequently create additional cost and work over time. Hold steadfast to the evaluation standards and process, though seeking assistance will become familiar with the standards and process. The result will be a stable enterprise infrastructure delivering enhanced performance, security and cost savings.

Scalability and delegation

All process must be developed with the scalability of the key deliverables. Process adoption and cultural change may take many months, and through rigor and consistency the organization will rise to excellence. As the organization rises to excellence, the process must be prepared to allow many staff to participate, allowing for the distribution of workload.

The technology review process is broken into three primary objectives: information collection, analysis of the information collected, and summary and actions as a result of the analysis. Resources can be allocated to support these primary business objectives. As bandwidth increases, the number of resources can easily be increased to provide optimal support.

- **Objective 1 information collection**: a group of business capture agents can collect business requirements, test the requirements, align functional requirements and other artifacts to be reviewed as part of the process. This is a critical step in the process, as a lack of information will have an impact on the entire process.
- **Objective 2 analysis of information collected**: the analysis of the collected information is easily delegated to multiple parties within the organization. The intent is it artifacts a review by various representatives together with the best feedback.
- **Objective 3 summary of the analysis**: the summary report is a collection of all comments received by the analysis process. The summary report, although often created by few individuals is in reviewed by all interested parties and feedback is solicited.

All three the primary processes are easily delegated to include multiple resources. When timelines require escalation, additional resources can be added intact timelines are not adversely impacted.

Technical analysis summary

Multiple variables exist when reviewing and implementing technological solutions. The review process is designed to work through the challenges by leveraging subject matter experts within the organization and vendor community. As discussed previously, the implementation of standards and the rigor to provide a consistent approach to evaluation will always serve the organization. Although, when open issues remain unresolved escalation to business owners may be required. The technical analysis summary document will assist in The identification of open issues within your proposed solution. Illustrated below is an example of a technical analysis summary table that can be easily integrated into a document found within the shared location in the organization. Some additional information in reading the technical analysis summary table provided:

- **Additional information.** Additional information is designed to assist the reviewer and business representative/owner with additional information related to the subject matter experts (SME) comments.
- **Appendix D3A**. A detailed appendix should be added to the technology analysis summary document to provide support and answers to commonly asked questions.
- **Fast track**. The fast-track column is a possible answer to the question. The format of the technical analysis summary document allows for a quick review of the solution by all interested parties and a history of all communication associated with the technology discussion.

Ref	SME notes, questions and comments	Additional information that may help you answer the concern	FAST TRACK: suggested answer
7.2.1	Does the solution use any form of protection for the solution service at the local facility? For example: services are replicated locally and remotely for availability and disaster recovery.	For example if the solution at the local site fails, what is the impact to the local site? Do the clients redirect to an alternate site?	Use appendix D3A - service replication for additional information. 4-21-09: the solution will leverage the same software to perform data service replication

The technical analysis summary should also include historical data and the resolution with a direct reference to the technical analysis summary document. An example of that table is listed below.

Ref	SME notes, comments, and questions	Response/completed
14.1 (7.2.1)	Does the solution use any form of protection for the solution service	4-28-09: Yes. Leveraging standard defined in appendix D3A.

All interested parties can review the active document change section of the technology analysis summary document. Leveraging the document change section will assist the review process by providing focus on items that have recently changed.

You prepared well, encountered some challenges along the way, and enjoy the peace and beauty of the open road. Away from the world, you and the road, basking in the success of the results you produced. The amount of rigor and discipline required to provide a successful road trip is also expected to build a technological solution. Enterprise infrastructure is no different.

Old-Fashioned Grit

We've discussed several important technologies and evaluation strategies targeted to produce an optimal enterprise infrastructure. All the processes and standards in the world will fail if the organization is not capable of delivering results. The strategy discussed herein allows an organization to place performance metrics around the various phases to drive accountability and results. Any process void of responsibility will have a challenge being successful, as all good things require effort and good old-fashioned work ethic and grit.

Value-add

All successful implementations must have the ability to "add value" to the recipient of the technology. Without value, the recipient will be less engaged and anxious to satisfy essential requirements for the success of the enterprise infrastructure. It is hopeful that recipients will understand the value-add to the entire lifecycle of the solution.

Building operational strength

The final phase of technical analysis for a business is to implement the solution. Many organizations have segmented reviewers, strategists, operational and maintenance labor pools. Survival within a segmented organization requires a clean "pass off" from the development and procurement activities to the implementation activities. The inclusion of cyber security must be overarching as the solution is implemented within the environment.

Enterprise architecture is the ability to provide a consistent computing environment to all customers. Persistent computing is a reachable goal, a level of excellence that is repeatable with every architecture design and rewarded by the excellence provided to those served.

Excellence in the enterprise

"We are what we repeatedly do. Excellence, then, is not an act, but I have it." Aristotle, 322 BC

We have come a long way, we've reviewed the strategy on standards and process, now we will focus on building excellence throughout the organization. Excellence is the reward for our rigor and commitment to the standards and process, we have fought the good fight we've endured the last mile.

Step 1: Define the direction

- Build a technical review document to develop a technology direction for your organization
- Implements active communication for all interested parties. The more reviewers and feedback, the better the solution. Build the direction, invite others to enhance the direction through feedback and comments
- Build a technical review process to develop technology direction for the organization.

- Organization discusses the solution as it relates to the four analysis criteria of enterprise architecture: functionality, performance, manageability, and fiscal accountability.

Step 2: Prioritize

Review the solution with an architecture decision matrix tool. The architecture decision matrix will assist in the alignment of business and strategic objectives to be weighted with financial responsibilities.

Step 3: Build standard solutions

Develop, socialize, maintain open standards that promote technology advancements and purchasing strength.

Step 4: Evaluate the solutions

Adopt a processor promotes a consistent, fair and open evaluation for all technologies. No exceptions for review should be granted, only accelerated timelines for urgent solutions.

Step 5: Produce results

- Provide scalability and delegation within the process implemented. The process must be able to leverage as many available resources as possible to be successful.
- Create "value-add" for the recipient of the technical analysis review process. Assist in the development of the preparation standards documents. Provide an implementation review once a solution has been purchased to promote consistency from the architecture to the implementation of the solution.

Step 6: Old-fashioned grit

- Provide consistency and discipline within the process implemented. The process will fail in the absence of discipline and consistency.
- Promote a new level of excellence. Enhance communication, drawings, styles and general perception of the service provided. Slowly through example, an adequate template, move the organization to a new level of excellence.
- Build an accountable customer experience. The strategies discussed herein are illustrative of many of the items

required to be successful. Once implemented, management and effective accountability (scorecards) will be needed to maintain the commitment to excellence that has been created. To achieve this in an enterprise management framework will need to be implemented. An enterprise management framework will impact the entire business process within the organization.

QRT – Aligning Technology and Business	
Summary of Aligning Technology and Business	Many technologies impact our effectiveness as businesses and organizations.
Complexity of implementation	This is the largest of the subsections within the book for a very specific reason, the complexity associated with cloud and local infrastructure requires careful thought and consideration.
Starting fresh	Collect inventory prior to building the system. Include a lot of detail. Many applications are in the market to assist with this process.
Modifying existing environment	For existing environments, in most cases, validating existing inventory is the first step. The next step is to organize your "IT system" based on existing business processes and deliverables, for example, email, database system, web services, and file storage.
Business Interruption	Minimal business interruption should occur.
Ballpark Pricing	Pricing is difficult for this subsection as it is very related to labor to collect and organize data. The collection of inventories for some organizations can be a substantial task. See *FTE or Contractor* for more information.
Learning Curve	There is a minimal learning curve. Understand where your inventory is and create systems based on your operational needs.

FTE or Contractor	System and components can be completed with an in-house resource or contracted. The collection of inventories does not require a lot of decisions throughout the process, making this an optimal activity for anyone with the desire to work. Once inventory has been collected, a different skill set may be required to organize the inventory into systems based on your operational needs.
Hints to get started	Start with the inventory that receives an IP address that includes standard IT infrastructure, as well as all other devices that may obtain an IP address from medical devices to industrial controls. Once you have mapped the inventory that receives an IP address, begin to map the attached devices, for example, storage or backup devices and add them as subcomponents of the primary component (the component that receives a direct IP address). Agents can be loaded on equipment to collect inventory information, or a manual accounting of all distributed IP addresses may be a place to start. Maintain data in a scalable and repeatable manner, for example, a database or spreadsheet. A great place to start is with the FedRAMP Inventory Template (see download section below). My preference is a visual map that will illustrate my inventory and their function within the environment.
Downloadable Tools	**Location:** https://goo.gl/joJuyf . **Filename:** NIST FIPS 199.pdf **Description:** NIST Data categorization publication 1- minute video on using the FedRAMP inventory collection tool (technical): https://youtu.be/WKeQaIGL3pk

Chapter 3: Cloud or Local Infrastructure?

The "Tree Gender Test"

Introducing new friends to the beauty of the forest is never absent from the "tree gender test." As you know, if you smell the bark of a ponderosa pine tree and it smells like vanilla the trees a female; otherwise the tree is a male. Many "tree gender tests" exist within the technology community, and certainly one of them is the introduction of cloud technologies changing the delivery model from the traditional IT to an "as a service" model.

picture 5

> "There are costs and risks to
> a program of action, but there are far less than the
> long-range risks and costs of comfortable in action"
>
> *-John F. Kennedy*

As with our "tree gender test," let's explore a few strategies for information technology environments:

1. **Defining success**: to get where you are going, we must first determine where we would like to be. We know many of our business challenges:
   - We have a lot of data; how can we continue to access this data effectively into the future?
   - As staffing vacancies increase, how can we find tune our operating expense as it relates to information technology?
   - Where do we get started in examining the different delivery models from traditional to cloud to

anytime/anywhere consumption of information and technology services?

2. **Security**: how do we secure and continually monitor threats and vulnerabilities in our information technology environments? The addition of an extended security boundary, like cloud technology, exasperates an already challenging problem.

3. **Aging Infrastructure**: aging infrastructure is a common reason to consider the move between local infrastructure and cloud infrastructure. Although, every business objective should be reviewed individually to line cost with functionality.

   - How long have you had your current equipment? Review carefully the cost of acquisition and maintenance related to your existing equipment, power consumption, bandwidth, and staff. This number is significant as it should be used as a comparison against cloud-based services. Remember cloud services charge based upon processing power, disk space, a random-access memory, and network bandwidth. Understand the cost completely.

Map Contour Lines

Several years ago, we were hiking around 10,000 feet with a group of 12 young men between the ages of 14 and 18. The young men reviewed the topographical map, aligned the compass and charted a path to our destination. We traveled through a small valley begin to conquer a steep incline that would take us up almost 2000 feet. We hiked along the rim of the mountain for several hours before our return to the valley floor. Revealed in a closer examination of our route, the young man failed to take notice of the density of the contour lines, which represent elevation change.

picture 6

Many computing environments understand the direction which they should take, although may misinterpret the "density of the contour lines." With the introduction of cloud technologies, advances in computer processing, storage, and memory, a closer review of our IT environment should cause us to reflect upon the objective we seek with technology.

Cloud technology adoption is filled with virtualization, public/multitenant and private/dedicated single tenant cloud environments, mobility and other organizational deliverables all available "as a service." As we look again at our compass and review the density of the contour lines of the map to guide us a longer journey, our IT journey contour lines may include a closer inspection of:

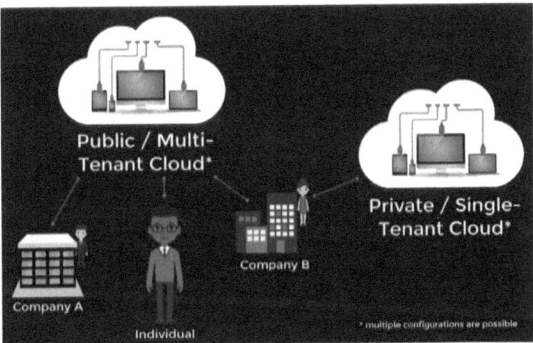

picture 7 - Public & Private Cloud

- **Operational Strength**: IT management will change as resources are, in some cases, geographically dispersed.

- **Virtualization/cloud**: cloud workload grounded formally in virtualization/hypervisor technology. How can we best leverage virtualization? Are all of the proposed workloads/applications within our environment conducive to virtualization?
- **Security**: with distributed workloads, what are our security controls that must be monitored in a geographically dispersed environment? How do we maintain the controls and continuously monitor for vulnerabilities?

Operational support may be frustrated as we move workloads to geographically distributed services. Illustrate clearly in the "as a service" delivery model: instead of managing a data center with multiple services (email, data, etc...), We are managing numerous relationships for services that satisfy organizational needs.

Planned correctly, an "as a service" model can be advantageous, although I submit that services within the traditional IT infrastructure are varied, with multiple support requirements. The multiple support requirements will not change with an "as a service" delivery model in most cases.

As we hiked up the hill, and back down the other side of the mountain, we returned to the same Valley we started in. Had the young man read the contours on the map correctly and consulted with his leaders, we may have saved resources and arrived at our destination hours earlier just as contour lines on the map, the movement to an "as a service" model may create costs and performance enhancements, as long as we are reading the "IT" map correctly.

In most cloud deployments, virtualization is leveraged. Often computer processing is referenced, although storage, network virtualization, and the size of the "pipe" to the Internet are also important variables to be considered. Although virtualization is the core of over 95% of all workloads residing in a cloud environment, not all virtualization platforms are created equal. Some considerations:

- **Co-Exist vs Migration?** For example, a KVM hypervisor will not work in a VMware ESX environment without considerable effort. Virtual machines access multiple resources to function properly, quickly "brokering" an enterprise workload from one hypervisor to a different hypervisor requires careful consideration.

- **Application latency** is often an unwanted surprise when migrating to a cloud infrastructure. Extended latency from the application to the back-end database in a geographically dispersed data center may cause the application to malfunction, and potentially the loss of data.
- **Application Modernization** is the review of your existing applications and measuring their compatibility with clod services. Often for organizations, this can be a challenging task as they need to first understand all their applications and the user of the application.
- **Security Boundary:** Your security boundary is extended with Cloud technology. Instead of your assets at one location, the assets may be spread over multiple locations.

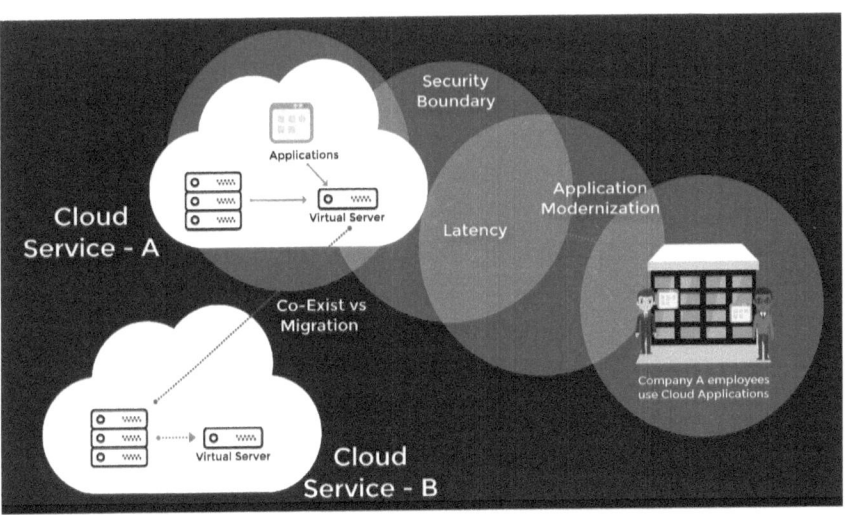

picture 8 - Cloud Challenges

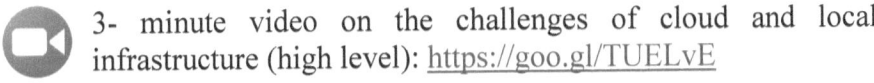 3- minute video on the challenges of cloud and local infrastructure (high level): https://goo.gl/TUELvE

Security controls our list of security standards that are related to specific hardware, software, process or any number of combinations within the IT environment to deliver a service (i.e.: email, file sharing, etc....). A control is documentation with a few key fields to establish what "right" looks like. Security controls within a group together to provide a security baseline for an organization, focused around the service to be delivered.

Exposed and Shallow Roots

The root of the tree is the primary artery supplying the tree with much-needed water and nutrients. The root of the tree extends deep beyond the surface to provide the strength required for the growth and long life of the tree. After completing several miles, our group found comfort in some shade provided by a field of trees. As our break was ending, we heard a loud crack in the distance. Upon further inspection, we discovered that trees were blowing over in the high winds. The roots of the trees were too shallow causing the trees to blow over easily.

Like an IT service, if we prepare the service and cannot gain the proper certification or security authorization to provide the service to our consumers, we have merely matured a service with exposed and shallow roots. The addition of security controls to any infrastructure, and indeed cloud infrastructure is an integral part of the process.

We quickly learned through experience with exposed and shallow-rooted trees, that we never wanted to sleep in a grove of shallow-rooted trees, as it only takes one tree to fall on you, to ruin a hiking trip. Unfortunately, with information technology the exposed and shallow roots of our decisions may be:

- Increased IT support cost
- Fewer resources to implement new technologies as the resources are consumed by maintaining existing infrastructure
- Fluid in rapidly changing security control requirements to an infrastructure that is not prepared.
- Adoption of new technologies, like cloud, without careful evaluation of operating and security cost.
- Security penetrations to the environment that are difficult to manage within the extended cloud security boundary.

Cloud Consumption and cost variables

Typically, in a cloud infrastructure, there are 3 to 6 variables that are used to evaluate price:

1. Virtual computer processing units often referred to as virtual CPUs.
2. Random-access memory often referred to as RAM. The amount of RAM assigned to a specific virtual machine.

3. Storage that is needed for the operating system of the virtual machine, applications, as well as storage space for backup and recovery operations.
4. (Private Cloud) Power required for all components that are part of the system hosted at the cloud provider that includes servers, storage, network.
5. (Private Cloud) Space required. Space is typically sold by the number of "U's" within the rack. Most data center racks are 48U.
6. (Private Cloud) Ping. Ping is referred to the bandwidth available within the environment. There's typically a bandwidth size that is defined, followed by a percentage of the defined bandwidth called "burst".

When purchasing public cloud services, the following information is helpful, although may not be part of your negotiation for cloud services.

Virtual Computer Processing Units (vCPUs)

A virtual CPU is a portion of the computing power from a single core on a physical processor. For example, a server may have two physical processors, within each of those processors you can have multiple cores. Let's say that each processor has four cores. A virtual CPU, dependent upon the workload, will consume a percentage of the processing power available within a group of processing cores. Dependent upon the hypervisor, the capacity may be five virtual CPUs per core, or in this example 20 virtual CPUs per physical processor, as the physical processor has four cores. This distinction becomes very important as your pricing out cloud solutions, as the industry tends to move between virtual CPUs and physical CPUs for pricing and licensing. Virtual CPUs are typically found within a cloud environment.

Virtual RAM (vRAM)

The amount of RAM assigned to a specific virtual machine (not to be confused with the virtual CPU, a virtual machine is a collection of one or more virtual CPUs) is a portion of the total available RAM found on the physical server. For example, a physical server has 64 GB of RAM. Each of the virtual machines on the physical server requires 8

GB of RAM, hence the physical server will be able to host a virtual machine. The amount of RAM used within a server is typically the variable that reduces the number of virtual machines that can operate on a physical host. The use of virtual RAM is generally found within a cloud environment.

A single physical CPU can support multiple VMs or services

Storage infrastructure

All cloud infrastructure and storage should provide the ability to perform replication, snapshots, and de-duplication to a geographically dispersed environment with multiple and varied timing increments. A geographically dispersed storage center should actively manage the data at a block level using real-time intelligence, providing fully virtualized storage at the disc level. Resources should be pooled across the entire storage array. All volumes within the storage array should be thin provisioned, and the data should automatically be moved between tears and RAID levels based on access and usage. Integrated space-efficient snapshots, then replication and dynamic business continuity software should be enabled within the cloud environment to provide high-availability of the storage environment.

High Performance / Transactional Cloud Services

A transactional application requires high IO's per second (IOPs) which needs to leverage high-speed disk in a fiber storage area network. A transactional database is typically a lot of very small, very fast read and write operations. From a computer perspective; the virtual CPUs and RAM required will be greater than that of other servers within the cloud environment. Processing power is key to transactional performance. Transactional applications use database structures like email, data analytics, and data warehousing.

File / Backup Cloud Services

A file dissemination/sharing, and backup/disaster recovery target often do not require many computer resources, and dependent upon the data load, may require slower disk resources. This is important because you can purchase more cloud capacity with lower performance. From compute perspective, the virtual CPUs and RAM required are minimal for these types of activities.

What type of data will be stored in the Cloud?

The type of data is broken down into multiple areas. Cloud options provide the ability to purchase different kinds of disk, performance values for those disks, and security related to the data.

- **Will the data be transactional**? Small, rapid read and write activity. Transactional data requires the quick placement of the information upon the spindle disk (disk write operation), coupled with rapid retrieval of the data (disk read operation). This type of data is typically served best within a fiber channel storage area network. Optimal performance should be around 100,000 IOPs.
- **Will the information be video or large images**? Video and large images are important to understanding as they will impact the compression ratio required for a site to site replication, as well as de-duplication of efforts needed for backup and recovery.
- **Will the data be office automation files?** These types of files include documents, spreadsheets, and presentations. The type of disk can be the most economical for these types of workloads.

What is the security required for the data?

For US Federal organizations or others that may be interested, NIST SP 199 does a great job at categorizing the level of security needed for your data. The standard for many environments is the protection of data in flight and data at rest, leveraging FIPS 140-2 security certification.

Data Security

FIPS 140-2 defines the security and encryption required for data at rest and data and flight. Data at rest is data that is sitting within your storage environment. Data in flight is data that is moved from the storage environment to satisfy an organization's requirements, replication, or backup activities; essentially it is data that is moving or in flight.

Encryption technology is required for the security of all data in flight and data at rest. FIPS 140-2 has three commonly used levels: level I, level II, and level III. Most environments are FIPS 140-2, level

II which is a software-based encryption requirement. FIPS 140-2, level III includes software-based encryption technologies as well as tamperproof hardware encryption.

Whether your organization uses FIPS 140-2 or another standard for data encryption, protecting the data within the organization is paramount to success, and frequently a decision factor between leveraging a cloud service or keeping sensitive data within the local infrastructure.

What services are critical to your operations?

When transferring services from a local infrastructure to a cloud infrastructure, business requirements should stay consistent. For example: if you are running an application at your local facility that can recover within five minutes, cloud technology should provide the same level of resilience. Too often, when organizations migrate to the cloud, it seems to negate the responsibility of information technologists to provide the same performance and functionality, which should not be the case.

A "service" is defined as a functional result of the computing environment. For example, email is a "service" which leverages an email server, storage, network bandwidth, backup and recovery software, and procedures. The "service" in this example is "email." The underlying requirements are defined as the technology that supports the service which includes the server, storage, software, process, and network.

At the root of all the technology, many decision-makers want to know the cost associated with maintaining a "service." When evaluating the differences between cloud and local infrastructure ask yourself what services are critical? I have asked that question 100 times, many, if not all have responded with "all services are critical." All services may be critical, although there is a direct cost associated with the word "critical service."

For example, I live in a cold part of the country that requires heat for six months out of the year. My home is equipped with a heating unit. If that heating unit fails, I understand that I may be wearing my jacket inside the house until a repair man is dispatched to fix my heater. The question I ask myself, is the heat in my home a critical service? I could equip my house with two heating units, at a considerable cost, but with the assurance that if one of my heaters fail, I always have a backup. For many of us though, installing a second heater in our home is cost inhibitive and is rarely done. We have accepted the fact and are willing to experience a level of discomfort for a brief amount of time in the event the heater fails.

Information technology and the delivery of services is no different. There is a certain level of risk associated with all services. The key is to understand the impact and appetite for absorbing the additional cost to increase the availability of the service.

Services are frequently protected by clustering or load-balancing hardware and software. Explore these options within the cloud as well as your local infrastructure and compare cost. An option may be to have your primary service hosted in a cloud, with a secondary service hosted at a local infrastructure.

The other variable to consider is the "time to recovery" of that service. Understanding the "time to recovery" is essential to enable the correct technology.

What data is critical to your operation?

To answer this question, you will need to be specific on the type of data used within your environment, whether that is a cloud or local infrastructure. For example, the organization may have a database that requires synchronous replication, whereas some training manuals may only need snapshot or backup technologies. The underlying question is, how much data can be lost?

Site to Site Replication – Asynchronous and Synchronous

The replication of data and services in a geographically dispersed environment that is more than 10 km apart has multiple questions that need to be answered. When you geographically disperse data, typically greater than 10 km, you must begin to consider

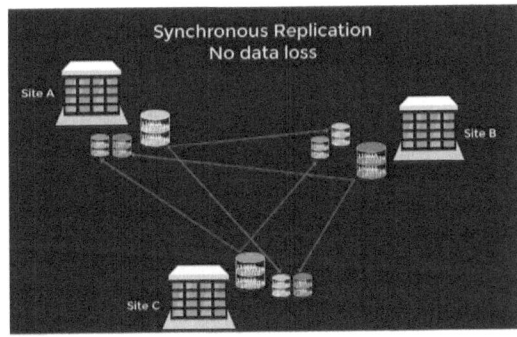

image 1 - Synchronous Replication

network bandwidth and associated limitations. Network bandwidth is interrelated to the type of data, the size of the data packet, and other variables. The loss of data can be addressed with three primary technologies: replication, snapshots, de-duplication/backup/recovery. Each of the fundamental technologies relates back to the priority of the data and services being replicated. There are two types of replication: synchronous and asynchronous. For example, my application writes data to a database. Before my application allows the transaction (the writing of the data) to be completed, it must receive confirmation for my database that the information was written successfully. In a replication model, synchronous replication means that the application will require confirmation from both the local database, as well as the geographically dispersed/remote database. The latency associated with writing the data to the geographically dispersed/remote location may create challenges for the application, so testing and validation is an important step.

The second type of replication is asynchronous replication. Asynchronous replication does not require a write confirmation from the replicated target, or in this example the target database. Hence, data can be written at the local site, and as bandwidth is available, data will be written to the geographically dispersed location. Although asynchronous replication reduces challenges with latency, it increases the possibility of data loss. If the primary site loses all data, any data that was scheduled to write to the "target/geographically dispersed site asynchronously" would be lost.

It is not uncommon to leverage both synchronous and asynchronous technologies. Frequently data will be synchronized

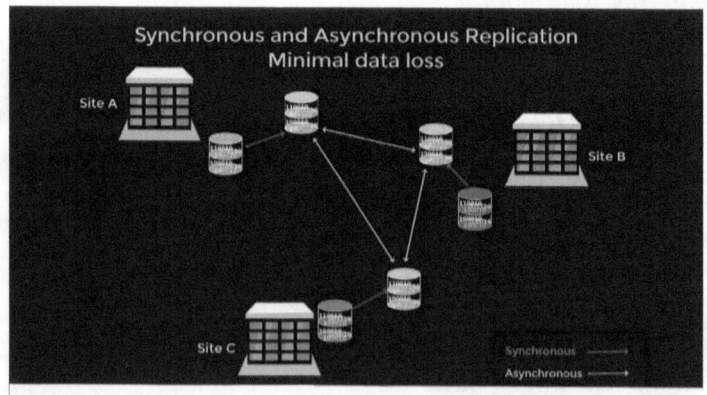

image 2 - Async and Sync Replication

locally within 10 km, and then asynchronously replicated to a geographically dispersed data center or cloud service.

Snapshot technologies

Snapshot-based technology continues to gain popularity for both cloud and local infrastructure, as the space requirement can be configured to be minimal. There are a few important things to remember about snapshot technologies.

1. Snapshots only store a pointer from a place and time. If the data within the snapshot changes, the changed data is written to the snapshot target before the new data is written to the production system, enabling the ability to "roll back" to a previous state of the data.
2. Snapshot technology can be both a hardware or software solution. The addition of hardware to complete snapshots allows for additional performance values typically not seen by software-based snapshot technology.
3. The snapshot target should always be defined as 100% of the actual data, although the data that resides at the primary location (the snapshot source, would have to change all the data at the same time to utilize all the data set aside at the snapshot target. Many environments reduce the snapshot target size to save cost. This is un-advisable. The savings associated with snapshot technology can be found in bandwidth utilization and performance.

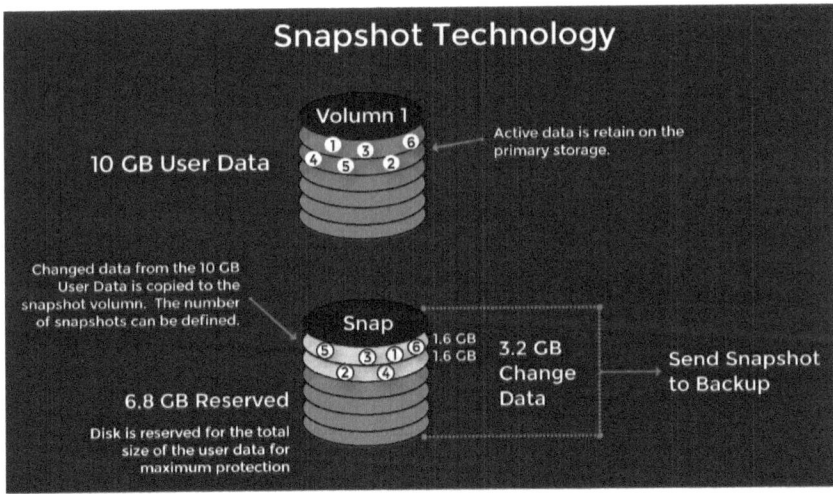

image 3 - Snapshot Technology

De-Duplication/Backup/Recovery

It is generally assumed that all data will receive the de-duplication, backup, recovery type technologies whether they are hosted in a cloud or local infrastructure. Although, some organizations may perform replication between geographically dispersed sites and only backup data at the geographically dispersed target site. There are several considerations:

1. reduction in data set size. Data de-duplication is replication friendly due to limiting the size of the data that we replicated as a de-duplicated payload. Payload represents the data set.

2. Certain data types de-duplicate more efficiently than other datatypes. It is not uncommon, to reduce the size of the backup payload by 60 to 80% (which is very dependent on the data type). Files that are text-based, some presentations dependent upon the content in the presentation, and spreadsheets perform well with de-duplication. Files that are large images for example do not leverage de-duplication technologies as well.

3. In a geographically dispersed environment, de-duplication is implemented before shipping the data over the network wire.

4. De-duplication is closely associated with backup and recovery technologies. It is not uncommon to de-duplicate data and then back up the de-duplicated data. Remember though, if you de-duplicate your data and then perform a backup, in the event of a restore of that data, you will need to restore the backup file and then rehydrate the de-duplication file to access the data, impacting restoration times.

Restoration of services and data

Backup and recovery activities are dependent upon storage availability and how fast the service needs to be restored. Many organizations have migrated to a disk to disk backup, with an archive to tape. The restoration of services leverages multiple technologies.

Does the service need to be restored in five minutes or 30 minutes or overnight? The time allowed to restore data associated with the service, whether it be in a cloud or local infrastructure, will define the type of technology required. If the organization needs restoration of the data, for example, within five minutes, a replication model will be necessary, and the physical location of the primary and target data sources will need to be evaluated. If the organization requires data within 30 minutes, we may be able to restore the data from backup or snapshots. In some organizations may be okay with data restoration within four hours or overnight.

The right size for backup

Not all data is created equally. Some data that resides within a cloud environment, providing a service like email, stores temporary data that may not require redundancy or a geographically dispersed site. For this data, local high-availability is an option. For example, the files on my desktop change at the rate of 1% daily. Meaning that, of the

image 4 - backup and recovery

1,000 files on my desktop, I will only modify or add ten files. The rate of change associated with cloud data, will define the amount of storage and backup resources required by the organization, also, the cost for the network bandwidth. Consider this: if my desktop has 100 files at 1 MB each, my total file size is 100 MB. If my rate of change is 10%, I will calculate that ten files at 1 MB each day will change. Hence my backup target must be able to accommodate the 100 MB of data when a full backup is performed. In addition, the backup target must have 10 MB per day for my incremental backups that are performed daily. Other variables will impact the actual target size requirement, such as de-duplication and archiving, but in general, this is the rule of establishing the disk size associated with backup activities.

Point in time recovery

Historically, point in time recoveries includes a weekly point, a monthly point, a quarterly point, a semiannual point, and an annual point of recovery. As data capacities have increased over the past ten years, organizations have reconsidered some of the standards. Using the example above, you can easily see that multiple copies of backup data can become quite costly. The reality is, 90% of our data is written once and never viewed or modified. As an organization you will need to find the balance between the cost of the capacity required to meet organizational needs and where does the data recovery become irrelevant.

Object and block-based storage

Management of the customers' data is critical. Although, the technology is changing rapidly. With the introduction of object-based storage, availability of information is an absolute, which differs from block-based storage. Without going on for pages discussing block and object-based storage systems, understand the basics that object-based storage quickly and efficiently distributes objects (data) to multiple locations by default. Object-based storage, accompanied by archiving, provides a point in time restoration without the need for many of the technologies discussed within this section.

Block-based storage, which is a standard for most organizations, leverages backup and replication technologies in blocks of data. You can adjust the size of the blocks, and other settings, although the core of the technology is to move blocks of data.

For example, it's a Friday evening, and you would like to stream a movie to watch in the comfort of your home. You could stream the video as the complete movie, which is a single "block" of data that would need to be transferred to your home, or, which is the standard, you could stream the movie as a collection of small data points, perhaps streaming five minutes of the film at one time. Downloading the entire film is an example of block storage. Streaming five minutes of the movie at one time is an example of object storage.

Cloud elasticity

An elastic capability is an ability for an organization to provide additional compute and storage resources. For many cloud providers, elastic capacity is available only when additional capacity is available from the cloud provider. If you intend to use flexible capacity, read the fine print as to the availability of this elastic capacity by the cloud provider you have selected. When evaluating your need for elastic capacity, perhaps leverage the following example as a template:

For my organization, 10% of our elastic requirements need to be satisfied immediately, whereas 90% of our elastic requirements can be fulfilled within 30 days. As an organization, we will define the disk type, memory and processing capacity needed for immediate elasticity as well as planned elasticity. Closely coupled with the increased capacity required for elasticity, is the amount of time the elastic expansion will be necessary.

For example, the organization on January 1 requires 100 virtual CPUs and 100 GB of storage as additional capacity to their 1000 virtual CPUs and 1000 GB of storage. The request for the elasticity was placed on November 1 of the previous year. The organization, starting on January 1 has 1100 virtual CPUs and 1100 GB of storage available. On April 1, the organization wishes to return to their standard operating size of 1000 virtual CPUs and 1000 GB of storage, returning 100 virtual CPUs and 100 GB of storage to the cloud provider. This example is a real-world example of elastic capability.

As a consumer of elastic resources, your price will reflect the cost burden placed upon the cloud provider. Think about the following: who pays for the hundred virtual CPUs and hundred gigabytes of storage that has been purchased by the cloud provider that is no longer generating revenue as of April 1. The cloud provider invests in additional capacity in November or December of the previous year, collects revenue between January and April, and has no income come April 1 for this purchased capacity expansion. Does the cloud provider have enough customers to float this additional capacity to another customer? Or does the cloud provider charge your organization the full amount over the four months of usage?

Cloud elasticity is one of many questions we have discussed within this section. Provided are some of the facts needed to make the right decision between cloud and local infrastructure. Ultimately, most organizations end up in a hybrid model with some resources as local infrastructure and others satisfied with cloud services.

Within this chapter, we have discussed multiple technologies to ensure that the service for the organization is available based upon need. Not all the services within your organization will utilize the same strategy for data and service recovery. The restoration of services and data for most organizations will not be a "one size fits all." To optimize the environment and cost refer to the chapter "systems and components" and define your systems, prioritize the systems, and allocate funding as appropriate to meet your organizational needs.

QRT – Cloud or Local Infrastructure	
Summary of Cloud or local infrastructure	Unfortunately, the decision of using cloud or local infrastructure is dependent upon multiple variables. The section has given you food for thought to arrive at the correct configuration for your environment. Historically, most situations are hybrid between cloud and local infrastructure.
Complexity of implementation	The largest of the subsections within the book for a reason, the complexity associated with cloud and local infrastructure requires careful thought and consideration.
Starting fresh	Collect inventory before building the system. Include a lot of detail. Many applications are in the market to assist with this process.
Modifying existing environment	For existing environments, in most cases, validating existing inventory is the first step. The next step is to organize your "IT system" based on existing business processes and deliverables, for example, email, database system, web services, and file storage.
Business Interruption	Minimal business interruption should occur.
Ballpark Pricing	Pricing is difficult for this subsection as it is very related to labor to collect and organize data. The collection of inventories for some organizations can be a substantial task. See *FTE or Contractor* for more information.
Learning Curve	There is a minimal learning curve. Understand where your inventory is and create systems based on your operational needs.
FTE or Contractor	System and components can be easily completed with an in-house resource or contracted. The collection of inventories does not require a lot of decisions throughout the process, making this an optimal activity for anyone with the desire to work. Once inventory has been collected, a different skill set

	may be required to organize the inventory into systems based on your operational needs.
Hints to get started	Start with the inventory that receives an IP address that will include standard IT infrastructure, as well as all other devices that may obtain an IP address from medical devices to industrial controls. Once you have mapped the inventory that receives an IP address, begin to assign the attached devices, for example, storage or backup devices and add them as subcomponents of the primary component (the component that receives a direct IP address). Agents can be loaded on equipment to collect inventory information, or a manual accounting of all distributed IP addresses may be a place to start. Maintain data in a scalable and repeatable manner, for example, a database or spreadsheet. A great place to start is with the FedRAMP Inventory Template (see download section below). My preference is a visual map that will illustrate my inventory and their function within the environment.
Downloadable Tools / Video	**Location:** https://goo.gl/joJuyf . **Filename:** NIST FIPS 199.pdf **Description:** NIST Data categorization publication 1- minute video on using the FedRAMP inventory collection tool (technical): https://youtu.be/WKeQaIGL3pk

Chapter 4: Container Technology

Container technology is an alternative to virtualization, although there are several things that need to be understood about this technology. In this discussion we will focus on the container  technology provided by Docker, as it tends to be a leader in the container space. We will explore the core technology associated with containers, as well as the comparison

picture 9 - Containers between containers and a hypervisor. There are some core differences between the technologies.

- **Communication** with the physical hardware. In both instances, communication between the operating system and eventually the application to the physical hardware is an absolute. The placement of that communication varies between containers and hypervisors.
- **Portability**. The placement of the communication to the physical hardware directly impacts the portability of the operating system and applications. Communication between the operating system and hardware in a virtual environment is dependent upon the hypervisor, whereas in a container environment it is 100% self-contained, giving it impressive portability.
- **Vulnerability remediation** is greatly enhanced within a parent/child inheritance model that is found within container technologies. Because containers are built upon a collection of "images" in a hierarchical manner, with a shared cache within the host, remediation to an image within any number of containers will ultimately remediate all containers with the shared image.
- **Configuration** can be accomplished via a text file within containers or saved as a state from a runtime environment allowing for maximum flexibility in the configuration of the container. Virtual machines have

similar functionality, although are dependent upon third-party products to accomplish this task.

Let's begin with the comparison between container technologies and hypervisor technologies. As I was growing up in the San Bernardino Mountains in the 1960s and 1970s, it was not uncommon to have a snow season lasted from Halloween to Father's Day. Snow could quickly drop in 8 to 12 feet, making life more challenging and fun all at the same time. Of course, we had four-wheel-drive vehicles. At that time to engage four-wheel-drive, you had to lock the hubs, which meant getting out of the vehicle and turning a large switch located on the front tires. Once completed, all four wheels would receive power from the engine. *The four-wheel-drive vehicle* is a lot like the multiple hypervisors available in today's market. The locking hub was powerful, although very specific to a car manufacturer. I could not use a Ford locking hub on a Chevy, just like I am unable to use a Microsoft Virtual Machine in a RedHat KVM Virtual machine environment. Container technology is a lot like all-wheel-drive vehicles; everything is self-contained. As I'm driving in an all-wheel-drive vehicle, granted not the same functionality as a four-wheel-drive vehicle, but similar in the

picture 10 – Locking Hub

aspect that when my tires slip, the other tires will engage to gain better traction.

This book is not a container book, although as we review use cases for our environments, the difference and similarities between containers and virtualization are key to current activities and planning for the future.

 1-minute video on Containers and Virtualization (non-technical): https://goo.gl/H4bLUz

Docker File

The Docker file calls the parent image, and associates in groups all the other images and dependencies required for the container to operate

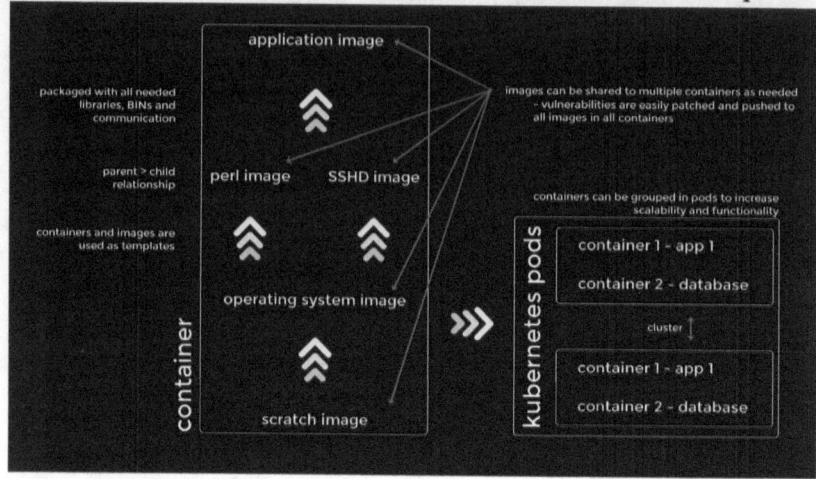

in the runtime environment. A lot of scripting is included in the Docker file to prepare the environment. The output from the Docker file is that it creates an image tree for the container to be formed.

Containers

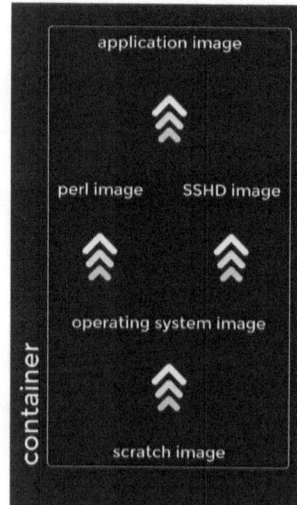

The container is a collection of images that are represented in a parent to child inheritance configuration. We start at the foundation of the container or the parent and build upon the foundational image to the application layer. The foundational image may be a "scratch image." Built upon the "scratch image" we will have an operating system, which is typically a bare-bones image. Commonly used for the operating system you may find Ubuntu, CentOS, and many others. The key is to keep the operating system lean focused on performance. On top of the operating system, we may add a language interface, for example, Perl and a security interface like

image 6 – Containers and PODS

SSHD, each represented as individual images, so that they can be used/shared with multiple containers. Note that we are creating libraries of images that can easily be used within any number of containers. The final image may be the actual application.

The individual container image can be grouped using Kubernetes into "PODS." "PODS" provide availability, (as noted in the image), also within the POD we can establish the environmental settings, volumes, configurations, ports and network communication. The key takeaway: when organizing containers and pods in the environment they should be 100% self-contained and extremely portable to any type of hardware (if the drivers to hardware are included in a container image).

Runtime environment

The runtime environment typically found on Linux kernel hosts the processes required to run the containers. The running of the containers themselves never pollutes the runtime environment. Remember, the container is 100% self-contained and leaves zero footprint on the runtime environment.

When hiking in the national forest, the Rangers will always ask you to "leave no trace." Leaving no trace means that you package all of your trash, clean up your campsite, and walk as not to create paths. Large groups of hikers often forget the walking part of "leave no trace." The process is easy; if you are hiking with ten other people, instead of following one another, you spread out horizontally as to represent single hikers instead of a group of hikers. We discovered that not only is it effective to "leave no trace" but allows you to see and share so many more experiences from the hike. One time when hiking with a dozen young men between the ages of 14 and 18, as we were walking in a leave no trace configuration, one of the young men discovered a bear off in the distance. Had we been traveling behind one another, most of us would've been looking at the pack of the person in front of us, just like the way a process runs a container within a docker environment. It is a leave no trace process.

Docker host

We have outlined the primary methodology associated with the creation of the container and how the runtime environment works for the container, as well as the ability to leverage the runtime environment to create the container itself. Now that we have the container built we understand how the container will function, how do we communicate and operate on the docker host?

The docker host leverages the "registry" as the list of available containers. The registry has a push poll relationship with the docker host, in addition, add a caching layer to optimize the movement of containers to the docker host. The "image cache" represents the container tree, although when running multiple containers, the docker host cache understands all images running on the host, and only loads the unique images for that specific container. In other words, as you run more containers within your environment, performance does not decrease. For example, you have ten containers running on a docker physical host. The allocation of memory and processing is an absolute whether you are using containers, core operating systems or a hypervisor. Each image within a container environment requires physical resources, such as memory and processing, as does a hypervisor. Within the ten containers you have ten child images per container or 100 additional images. As the registry loads container number one onto the docker host, container number one possesses 90 of the 100 additional images required for the remaining containers. As containers two through 10 are configured to run they will access the image cache instead of pulling new images, saving 90% of your workload. A great illustration memory loss can be performed on your desktop operating system. Turn off your desktop, turn on your desktop and without opening any applications document how much RAM is being used. For this example, let's say that you have 4 GB of RAM, and as you boot the system you have 3.4 GB available, or .6 GB is in use. Open a word processing or email application. Return and document the available RAM on your system after opening your application. For this illustration, let's assume that you now have 3 GB of available RAM, or 1 GB of RAM is in use. Close your application and turn off your desktop. Turn on your desktop and document the available RAM, without opening any applications. You will notice that instead of having 3.4 GB available, you may now have 3.3 GB available, as the operating system has consumed .1 GB of RAM for residual "pollution" left within your operating system. This unfortunate occurrence can run true for a hypervisor as well. A container environment, because it loads nothing in the runtime environment, has zero residual pollution.

The docker host also loads networking and storage volumes, as well as an API for the docker client. The storage volume within a docker host allows for persistent storage in the environment. As discussed, containers 100% self-contained, hence any data written within the container would be destroyed when the container is destroyed. The use of persistent storage allows for containers to write information to the docker host that is retained within the storage volume, regardless of the state of the container by which it was created.

Docker Client

The Docker client creates a push poll relationship with the docker host/registry to access the containers, creates/runs/commits containers, and configures the hardware as needed as it is related to networking and storage.

Use Case: Containers in a Virtual Machine

Containers in a virtual machine allow for the easy adoption of container technologies, while slowly introducing the customer into the new technology with minimal business impact. Illustrated below is an example of an application that leverages PODS, Containers and a Virtual Machine to deliver their solution. Very innovative use of container-based technology.

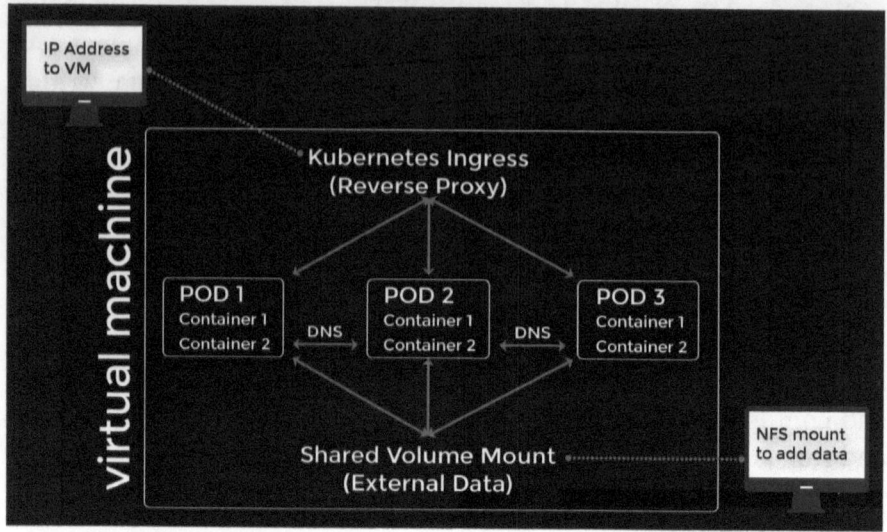

image 8 - Containers and Virtual Machines

Kubernetes can provide an XaaS feature, but it can be challenging without using a few tools available. These tools can provide better management to deploy your apps using the power of Kubernetes to organize them among the provided servers better. The image has an example on how Kubernetes will manage to deploy your apps with the given distribution of its cluster. Important Note: The image below shows projects apps divide equally among the nodes, though this is possible to happen, kubernetes will not always reserve one node per project, it will spread apps among all nodes according to the resources available and the apps requirements. This example shows 3 projects (Web Project A, Web Project B and AI Project A) each one of them uses different technologies on their apps, for instance, Web Project A has a Java app and Web Project B a Ruby on Rails app. Here we are using Helm to manage these projects, helm is a tool built for kubernetes that help us deploy and manage all the necessary configuration and requirements for our apps. With helm we can achieve granularity and can divide our deployments into different environments for the same app. Important Note: We must use the 12 factor rule to achieve such level of granularity. Kubernetes can reserve resources according to the app needs, for instance, on our Web Project A we've requested 4GB of Ram and 2 CPUs Cores for our Java app, kubernetes will only deploy this app on a node that has sufficient memory and cpus available to accommodate that app requirements. Kubernetes has lots of features including one where you can specifically set the node where it will deploy your app, it will fail if the resources are insufficient. Another resource allowed to be reserved is the Storage, on our example we have a glusterfs cluster configured with 1TB available, on Web Project A our Postgres database requests for 100GB of Storage so we can, with the proper configurations, reserve a persisted storage for our database. Kubernetes supports a variety of storages, you can check the list here.

Use Case : Deploying as a XaaS

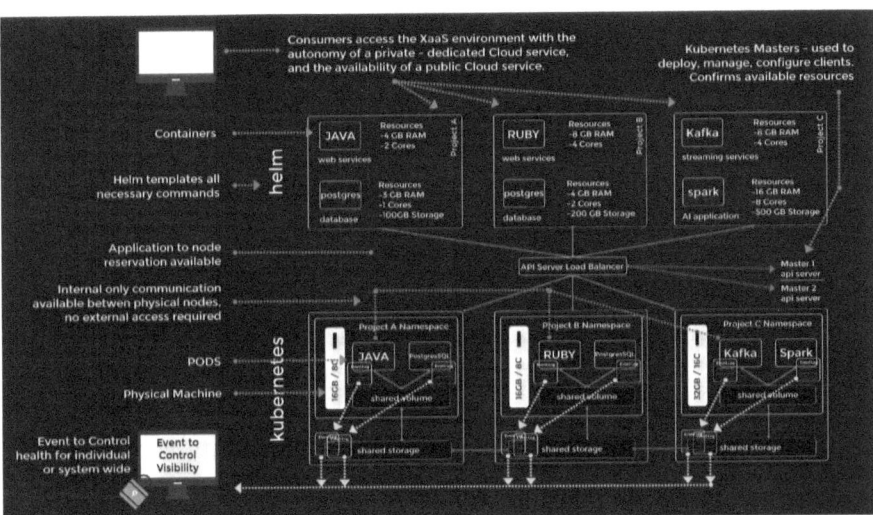

image 10 - XaaS Offering

The above image represents a potential use case for container technology within a public or hosted (private) infrastructure.

Kubernetes or Docker Automation

Google Kubernetes typically perform management of the docker containers and automation between the containers. Docker has an automation platform as well, although most environments tend to lean towards Google Kubernetes. Kubernetes allows for scripting to automate the movement of data and processes within the container environment. Illustrated below is an actual container environment that can be used to provide infrastructure and platform as a service to consumers. To provide infrastructure or platform as a service with the container environment takes advantage of many of the things we've already discussed. Additionally, some things to consider:

- Look into the "12 factor application" methodology (https://12factor.net) when developing applications will run as a service.
- Kubernetes will require additional software to assist with the management of projects as they are delivered "as a service". Granularity is required to divide the deployments into different environments. "Helm" (https://heml.sh) is a package manager for Kubernetes.
- Reserve resources for applications must be included. This includes the ability to "not boot" a container with inadequate resources.
- Establishment of persistent storage and the resources associated with that storage. For example, GlusterFS cluster may be configured and reserved by different tenants within the system.
- Flexibility to establish a multimaster or single master environment dependent upon demand. Kubernetes has an API service running on the master(s). The API is secure with TLS protection and only those, except for the nodes and proper user access will have the ability to Kubernetes administrative function.
- Will the environment be configured as high-availability (multiple masters)?
- Communication is critical as containers reside on different physical hardware and possess different logical namespaces. As a result, in internal network DNS, on access to the external world will be required as well. "Kafka" works well with Kubernetes clusters.

Qualifying questions for the Environment

- What is the OS that will be on the Docker Host?
- What is the targeted OS's for the Docker images?
- Who will build the Kubernetes and Docker environment from bare metal?
- Will clustering be required?
- Will the installation occur on physical "hosted" servers or a Kubernetes / Docker environment built on a cloud service like AWS?

- During the build, configuration and management phases, will SSH access be available OR will the management of the environment be at the hosting facility?
- Will the environment support vertical scaling?
- What is the desired File Service? (NFS, GlusterFS, etc..)
- Does the environment have a Load Balancer configured? Will a load balancer be required for the Kubernetes / Docker environment?
- Is there a firewall protecting the environment OR will a firewall be required?

Qualifying questions for administration and security

- Who will manage the environment?
- Will the environment be configured at the same location that the environment will be hosting services? This is a substantial concern for the configuration of the environment. It is suggested that the environment is configured at the location it will be hosting services.
- Is all access to the environment blocked by default? Kubernetes works with role-based access (RBAC) to provide access to multiple users at different levels.

QRT – Containers	
Summary of Cloud or local infrastructure	Containers are an effective method for providing information environments, although can be complicated and certainly different than "traditional" and "cloud" based technologies. Most of the apprehension to adopt containers is based in "the unknown". Too often we deploy technologies that provide us with a level of comfort, and the move to container technology, for many, does not provide the comfort needed.
Complexity of implementation	Containers can be a challenge for many environments. Although, once the container environment has been established and the automated put in place, containers are no more difficult than any enterprise infrastructure.
Starting fresh	Start with containers and use containers as the core infrastructure for everything you can in the environment. A

	hybrid model between containers and virtualized systems will prove to be more expensive.
Modifying existing environment	Look at the services within your environment that can benefit from a scalable compute model. Perhaps start with non-data centric services.
Business Interruption	Dependent upon your environment, containers can be disruptive. For an existing environment, start the containers while maintaining your current environment. Slowly migrate and become familiar with containers.
Ballpark Pricing	Pricing is difficult as it varies based upon your need and the container technology used. It is no uncommon to experience a cost savings when shifting to containers. Other factors are important when calculating cost: service availability, security of the environment and service/data isolation and spillage.
Learning Curve	There is a learning curve with containers. The concept will be easy for a virtual machine engineer to understand.
FTE or Contractor	Containers can be easily completed with an in-house resource or contracted.
Hints to get started	Research the container technologies available in the marketplace and the automation that accompanies the container technology. Remember that the container can be one vendor and the automation to operate the container environment can be multiple software technologies. For example: Many organizations use Docker Containers managed by Google Kubernetes.
Downloadable Tools/Video	1-minute video on Containers and Virtualization (non-technical): https://goo.gl/H4bLUz

Chapter 5: Using Technology for Business

Making homemade pizza requires multiple ingredients like basil, tomatoes, cheese, and dough. As individual ingredients (or components) they may taste different than when put together in a pizza. As the pizza comes out of the oven (the pizza is a collection of the ingredients) the taste of the pizza emerges, complimenting the individual ingredients.

picture 11

The use of technology within our environment is like that of a pizza. The components include the hardware like servers, storage, networks and desktops as well as the software, operating systems and cybersecurity products. The elements of technology (like the ingredients of a pizza), when placed together form a system, that ultimately should complement one another. Here lies in the challenge. For many organizations technology and cyber technologies are moving at a pace that is too difficult to understand. A base understanding of the related technologies will assist in the proper decisions related to the system. The content of Chapter 2 is designed to give you exposure to key technologies, typical questions, and answer, as well as other vital information to make the correct choices related to the ingredients that form your technology systems.

The outcome of your decisions as it relates to technology and cyber have an impact on profitability, protection of intellectual property, and a myriad of other efficiencies designed to fine-tune your organization. Just like the ingredients of your homemade pizza, once you understand some of the components that comprise your technical and cyber infrastructure, you will see that it's not that difficult.

 1-minute video on pizza and IT systems (non-technical): https://youtu.be/d3DWJSkmuF8

Systems and Components

A system is a collection or unification of "like" technologies to satisfy a stated objective. In other words, when you choose to send your email message, the email server, the network switch and multiple software products are activated to send the message (image 1).

The relationship between components within the organization is rarely isolated to a single system (for example the email system), in fact, there are core components that impact multiple systems and in some cases all systems within your organization.

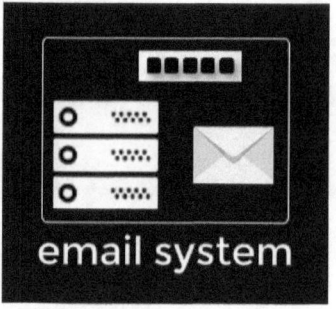

image 11

The relationship between your components that make up your systems, or deliverables like email, is critical when decisions are required to optimize cost, enhance cyber security as well as other efficiency-oriented tasks. For example, in addition to your email system you have a database and file sharing system. Each system has different components, although share the same network component. A change to the network infrastructure may have an adverse impact on all the associated systems, in this example the database system and the filesharing system. The relationships extend far beyond the enterprise infrastructure and have a direct impact on your ability to secure the environment properly.

Understanding the systems within your organization is a key task that must be completed before you can declare that your environment is secure. We have discussed the definition of a system, which is a collection of components. In the cybersecurity world, the system is comprised of the server, storage, network, operating system and software that supports a business objective (see image 1). Cybersecurity controls are grouped into cybersecurity baselines or frequently referred to as polices, compliance or authorizations.

Controls

The cybersecurity controls, grouped as baselines, are specifically associated with the system (for example: email). The cybersecurity controls address the software, hardware, location, people and process associated with the system.

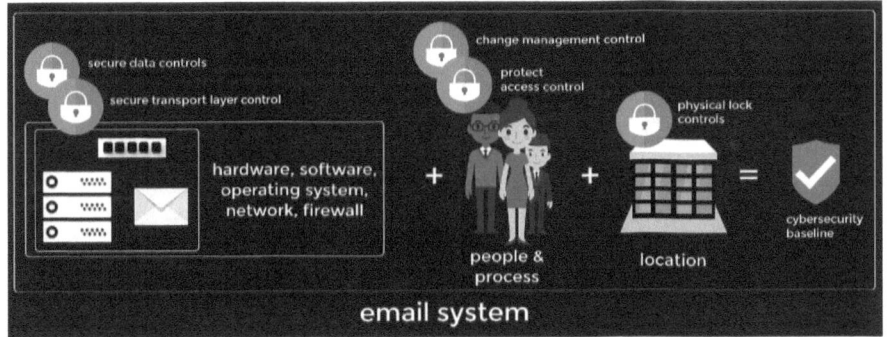

Image 2 illustrates multiple cybersecurity controls used to support the email system. Note that some of the cybersecurity controls are hardware, software and operating system focussed, while others may focus on non-technical components in the system, for example people, process and location. All of the controls and information related to the delivery of email for the organization is collected into the cybersecurity baseline.

Weights and Priorities

It is not enough to monitor or manage the security based upon components within the system; you must monitor the impact of all components within the system based upon weights and priorities. Each event that occurs in an environment means something different when all the events are put together.

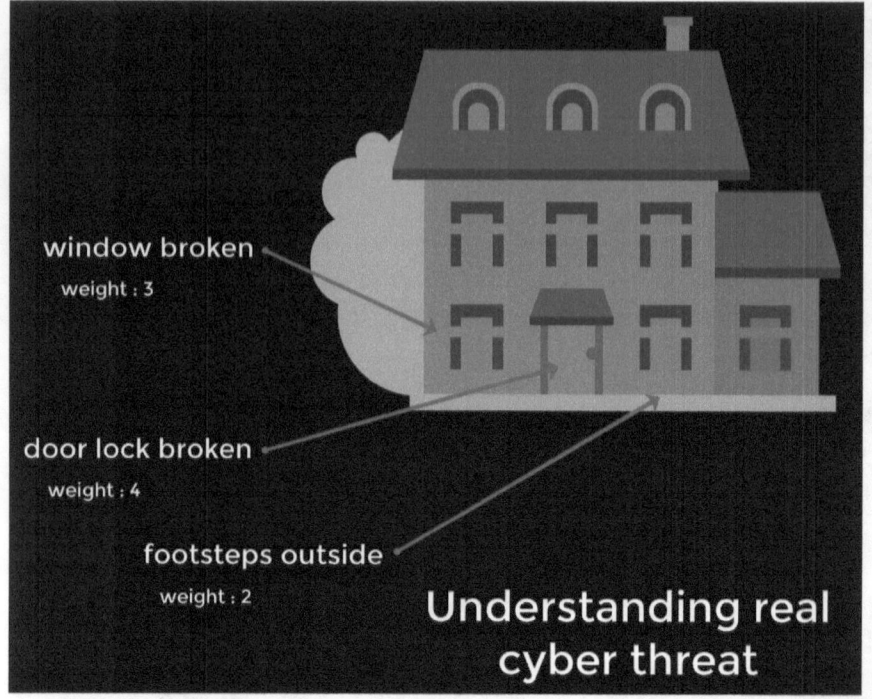

window broken
weight : 3

door lock broken
weight : 4

footsteps outside
weight : 2

Understanding real cyber threat

image 13

The cyber threat is calculated upon the cumulative risk associated with the "system." All cyber threat impacts the environment differently. Hence the level of danger, as well as the related threat to other components in the environment, are all variables to consider.

For example: If a secure home is an objective, the "system" is the house, the "risk weights" derive from the windows, doors, and footsteps. If we declare low risk as a weight of 0-3, moderate risk as a weight of 4-7 and high risk as a weight of 7-10, what is our actual cyber threat when multiple events occur? Individually the activities are low to moderate risk: Window was broken: 3, the Door lock was broken: 4, Footsteps outside: 2.

If all events occur, the cumulative risk is high, with a total weight of 9 (3+4+2). A focus on individual components in the environment is essential, although it provides a limited view of the actual threat in the atmosphere. The view must be expanded to include the entire system, the cumulative total of all consistent threat.

 50 second video on house and weights (non-technical):
https://youtu.be/dANuzjxP8MA

Building a Persistent Computing Environment

Building an architecture to provide a persistent computing environment requires thought, discussion, and action. The following pages will give several examples of persistent computing technologies designed to provide a service environment for all business use cases. Applications (services) hosted in an enterprise environment require different levels of availability (persistent computing). Technologies that are part of a persistent computing architecture include:

- **Services**. Technology today allows for services (for example email, web service and file shares) to be available always. Rarely should service be unavailable for more than 30 minutes that includes, and not limited to, rapid restoration of the environment in the event of a failure.
- **Backup**. Now that we can recover a failed piece of hardware, we must be able to access historical data predictably at the application layer. The ultimate objective returns the hardware and software to acceptable service levels.
- **Data**. Preparation for data access challenges at specific geographically dispersed locations must be discussed within a persistent computing environment. Remember, all data is not created the same; hence different strategies may apply.

Persistent computing architecture is dependent upon all technologies and costs to be successful. The relationship between a service, the data, and backup activities define experience received by the user. It is important as you begin to understand your persistent computing needs that you define the technologies and processes that will be part of your persistent computing environment. I have presented three examples: services, backup, and data.

Once you have defined the technologies that are part of your persistent computing environment, we need to breakdown the available technologies and group them under the urgency of the technology to the environment. Some services will always need to be available whereas others can be restored within 24 hours. Understanding the business need, exploring the available technologies to satisfy that need, balanced with cost and business impact, are good steppingstones to arriving at a persistent computing architecture that is both functional and cost-effective.

Now that we have a few of the persistent computing objectives defined (services, backup, data), let's begin grouping the technologies to support the objectives by the following levels of urgency:

- **Basic**: represent core standards, for example, imaging and the rapid recovery of services. Bring the service online consistently every time.
- **Standard**: flexible and cost-effective technologies designed to offer excellent support and persistent computing alternatives.
- **Critical**: absolute availability is required. Flexibility may be sacrificed to ensure service and data availability at all cost.

Taking the three primary technologies, we've identified as part of our persistent computing environment (services, backup, and data), let's apply proposed technologies to meet our urgency associated with the business need.

- **Services** may have the following associated persistent computing technologies:
  - **basic**:
    - static recovery
    - network operating system streaming
    - static virtualization
    - boot from storage/SAN
    - dynamic recovery
  - **standard**:
    - service replication
    - network load balancing
  - **critical**:
    - clustering
    - network load balancing appliances
    - type I virtualization with dynamic image movement
    - automated workflow virtualization
    - grid computing
- **Data** may have the following associated persistent computing technologies:
  - **basic**:
    - raid

- o **standard**:
  - host replication (local/remote)
  - snapshots
  - clones
- o **critical**:
  - array replication (local/remote)
- **Backup** may have the following associated persistent computing technologies:
  - o **basic**:
    - backup to local media
  - o **standard**:
    - backup to local media
    - data de-duplication
  - o **critical**:
    - MAID technology (long-term storage)
    - Archive

The technologies of replication and restoration

Understanding some of the basic technology that supports persistent computing is essential to deciding about the technology that will match your business requirements.

Breaking down the myth of replication

Asynchronous and synchronous replication enable the movement of data from one site to another. Asynchronous replication allows the process to continue regardless of the secondary site ability to write the data, whereas synchronous replication will wait for the secondary site to write the data before completing the transaction. There are several questions you may want to ask yourself before selecting the type of replication to use within your organization. Many organizations use a mixture of both asynchronous and synchronous replication-dependent upon the applications needs and the business/organization requirements.

The difference between asynchronous and synchronous replication can often be milliseconds as it relates to the writing of the data at both sites in normal operational environments. Although we need to be cautious to not excuse the reality that asynchronous replication has the potential of losing data, in the event the secondary site, often referred to as the target site, becomes unavailable for any number of reasons, and a failure occurs at the primary site.

One of the primary challenges to deploying asynchronous replication model is the bandwidth requirement between the geographically dispersed sites. For example, my primary site resides in Tucson Arizona, and my secondary site lives in Lincoln Virginia. The number of "network hops" between Tucson and Lincoln, coupled with the bandwidth available, will be critical factors to the performance of the application at the primary site in Tucson Arizona. Remember, if you select synchronous replication, which guarantees the data in Tucson and Lincoln will be the same, may take 1000 milliseconds to confirm that the data has been written successfully at both sites. The 1000 milliseconds will be presented as performance related challenges within the application. Sometimes, the cost from a performance perspective for synchronous replication may be unacceptable to an organization, although there are alternatives.

Use Case: The confirmation of the data been written synchronously in Tucson and Lincoln is critical for the organization. If the primary site is damaged, attacked or destroyed, Tucson wants to ensure that the data is available in Lincoln. The critical application and data within Tucson reside on a server called TUCAPP1. All the information is replicated synchronously to a server in Lincoln called LINAPP1. Adding a third server to this configuration will significantly enhance performance with minimal risk to the organization, in this example, we will call it TUCAPP1b. TUCAPP1 will synchronously replicate data to TUCAPP1b. TUCAPP1b will asynchronously replicate data to the Lincoln server, LINAPP1. The benefit to this configuration is that Tucson performance will improve, as synchronization occurs within the Tucson network. It is suggested that TUCAPP1b is separated the maximum distance to avoid natural disasters to the data center, although it should be restrained to the Tucson local area network. In the rare occurrence that the entire Tucson facility is destroyed, data could be potentially lost between the asynchronous activity of TUCAPP1 and LINAPP1.

The one to many replication models allows for the critical source of data to be written at multiple locations. Often enterprise environments will write the data to the local site and then to a remote site, as we have discussed in the use case surrounding Tucson Arizona and Lincoln Virginia. A server can be synchronously replicated to ensure optimal access to critical data while running as a parallel process, data can be replicated to a geographically dispersed site to guard the data against catastrophic failure at the primary site, in this case, Tucson Arizona. The flexibility available with host-based replication allows for the enterprise to be creative based on resources and funding while maintaining the availability of services that may depend on storage. Some of the key questions associated with replication may include:

1. How long can the organization be without access to specific data?
2. What is the distance between the source or primary site and the target or secondary site?
3. How many network "hops" are between the two sites?
4. How much data can be lost in the event of a recovery?

Many software providers include host-based replication software for data and services. The replication of data is essential, although, without the appropriate services, the data alone may not provide what the organization requires.

The replication of services is defined as the ability to have a service running at the source site, and upon failure, the services are restored at the target site. The rough order of magnitude cost associated with the replication of services and data at the software layer is $1200-$4000 per server. When compared with other persistent computing options, service and data replication at the host layer is the least expensive and most comfortable to deploy.

Rollback

Do you remember the old phrase "garbage in-garbage out"? This simple phrase is a variable for decisions related to replication. If the primary site is infected, for whatever reason, the data replicated to the secondary site or target site may also be affected.

Rollback enables caching for a "rollback" to a last known good state. For example, it is discovered that all replication data from noon on Friday, 12 December was compromised or contaminated. All sites, local and geographically dispersed, would roll back to a date sometime before 12 December. The frequency of the rollback cache will change based on business policy and requirements.

Rollback cache allows for greater flexibility in preserving a persistent computing architecture. In the absence of rollback cache, restoration is often initiated through a backup solution in the environment.

Recovery versus service availability

Recovery and service availability, although very similar in function are two distinct technologies that are important to understand. Many of the solutions for persistent computing architecture are based on the recovery of service or availability of that service.

Availability of the service: the availability of service refers to the failover of service and the service being covered, typically on an alternate server or virtual machine. The availability of a server should be quick, usually within milliseconds. Technologies that enable the availability of a service include clustering, virtualization and service replication. As a reminder, a service is the byproduct of the hardware, software and operating systems established in your environment that "serve" your consumers, for example, email, file sharing, and application access.

Recovery of a server: the restoration of a server typically refers to the rebuild of a failed server. Technologies that enable the recovery of a server include, a static image recovery, dynamic imaging, type II virtualization and network operating system streaming.

Local versus remote: the tolerance of an application

As you develop an architecture to support a persistent computing environment, you will need to understand the difference between a local and a remote site. The distance to the remote site, or sites, is critical as several technologies are restricted by distance. Distance is important as it directly relates to the amount of time it takes for a packet of information to write to the remote site and the direct relationship to the tolerance within the application.

Static and dynamic imaging

A static image provides the ability to restore a failed service. Some of the objectives accomplished with imaging include:
1. Restore a service consistently
2. Restore the service with little to no knowledge of the service provided
3. Restore the service in less than 30 minutes.

The primary difference between static and dynamic imaging solutions are cost and the time allowed to restore services.

Static imaging: the rough order of magnitude cost is typically less than $300 per server. Static imaging captures an image at a "point in time". For example, I have a maintenance window that dictates all my servers are "captured" (which requires the server to be off-line) on the first of every month. If a failure occurs that requires me to use a static image, I re-provision the server to the most recent "point in time" static image. Some considerations:

- Servers must be taken off-line to capture. This can be done in a 20 to 60-minute process dependent upon the server configuration.
- Once the image has been restored, it may take an additional 3 to 4 hours to update security and patches.
- "Like-hardware" may be required. For example, server manufacturer ABC fails, replacing the server with manufacturer DEF may not work. There are some exceptions and optimization that can be done to accommodate the restoration to "unlike hardware."

Schedule dynamic imaging: the process here is to capture the image (as with static imaging) and provide scheduled updates, for example, every four hours. This too will require "like hardware," unless additional drivers are placed on the image to allow it to run on "unlike-hardware successfully".

Real-time dynamic imaging: the ability to update the image in real time. As soon as a byte on the production server changes is automatically updated on the image server. Also, to the "real-time" update of the image, the capture is file-based, typically facilitating immediate restoration to any hardware platform.

Network operating streaming

Network operating streaming, in concept, has been in the technology community for many years. The simple idea of loading the operating system and application into random-access memory is at the core of computing. With a basic understanding of streaming technology, let's review the strength this technology has within an enterprise environment. In the event of a failure or the need to take a server off-line for maintenance, another server can be booted in its place, all in the time it takes to Buddha server. The technology is very similar to a technology found within storage environments called "boot from San" leveraging LUN masking to convince a server's HBA card that the boot partition on the SAN is LUN0. A few differences between boot from San and network operating system streaming is versatility, cost, and dependencies.

It is important to note the concept of a "base" image, allowing for the deployment of "read-only" and/or "read-write" network operating systems. In a server environment, most of the images are deployed as read/write images, as a server image can be very dynamic. A consideration for the read-only server may be an application server in a network load balanced cluster, where consistency of the network server is a success factor. Once the network operating system has been streamed to the server, services continue to run from random-access memory. The network operating system streaming services is typically below $800 per server.

Virtualization

Virtualization is divided into two primary types within the x86 environment: type I and type II. The difference can be found in the location of the virtualization environment. Virtualization that is focused on performance is typically a type I virtualization, whereas testing and workstation type of virtualization generally is type II.

Type I virtualization (bare-metal/native)

Type I virtualization is the most common virtualization scene to host production and performance-oriented applications within a data center. One of the primary advantages to a type I virtualization is the ability to provide high availability of services within the enterprise infrastructure. Type I virtualization is typically hosted on a shared storage system, frequently found on storage area networks for performance, scalability, and flexibility. The virtualization software installs as a "hypervisor" that establishes a relationship with the hardware and drivers associated with the physical host or server.

Type I virtualization does not replace the need for an operating system, it simply virtualizes the hardware host. For example, an organization may have one physical server, although would like to create three different servers. In the absence of virtualization, the organization would have to purchase three physical servers. With the introduction of type I virtualization, three virtual servers can be hosted by this single physical server, providing the organization with three virtual servers, that will act and perform very similar to three physical servers.

Type II virtualization (hosted)

Type II virtualization is often available for free within the information technology community. The functionality of a type II virtualization is very limited and is often used for testing and development activities. Type II virtualization provides a very functional "static restoration" alternative within the persistent computing architecture, although is rarely used. It is important to note that capturing a virtual image as a "rollback" alternative can be a challenging task.

Dependent upon the server and storage resources multiple operating systems can be enabled on a single hardware platform. Virtualization is a great way to reduce physical servers within the environment, although historically is not always a cost saving. Dependent upon the application and number of servers needed, as well as the virtualization features you would like to embrace for your organization, virtualization may only add a management and security challenge that you may not be prepared for.

Data duplication

Data de-duplication coupled with the site replication enables the elimination of physical tape media and libraries. The replicated data set is considerably less than the native data set when leveraging de-duplication technologies. De-duplication technologies use compression algorithms to optimize the amount of data to be replicated or backed up. It is important to note that data de-duplication can work miracles in an environment, with up to 75% reduction of data size for replication and backup, although it is not a guarantee. Different types of data, for example, small text files versus large images will perform differently within de-duplication technologies. If looking at making a de-duplication investment, take samples of all of your data and carefully review the compression ratio that occurs following the de-duplication activity.

Dependent on regulation and policy, tape may be required, although can be completed at a central site. Elimination of tape brings many efficiencies, cost savings, performance, and reliability that traditional tape backup and restore have consistently fallen short on delivering.

De-duplication is often an appliance within the enterprise environment. Some common concerns about a non-appliance-based de-duplication include:

De-duplication is most efficient when de-duplication occur for all data in the environment. For example:

- Some solutions perform data de-duplication dependent on the storage volume or host. If similar data is stored in two different volumes, de-duplication of the same file in different volumes may not occur.
- Compression must occur on de-duplicated data to increase efficiency.
- Performance overhead must be considered and monitored closely. Many vendors claim a 3 to 4% performance degradation when de-duplication activities are occurring, although many customers have reported up to 30 to 40% performance the degradation.

Archiving

Archiving is a process primarily driven by automated workflow and business defined roles to manage data within the enterprise storage environment. Redundant file elimination and redundant block elimination are essential to a successful archiving solution. The ability to store "like files" as a single instance can be a cost savings associated with the technology.

Archiving is a complementary technology to data de-duplication. Remember that archiving will address storage needs for active data, whereas data de-duplication addresses the backup data.

Archiving functions on a technology that places "stubs" to find the archive data. For example, I have a file called Sparky.Doc, and it is stored on the primary storage. When stored in an archiving solution, a single copy of Sparky.doc is retained, while duplicate copies of the file are saved as "pointers" to the original file.

The Sparky.doc file resides on server A. This file can reside as a "file" or an "attachment" to an email message. The Sparky.doc file is also available to the server B. Team members on server a and server B can review the Sparky.doc file, although the actual "file" Sparky.doc is only stored once on the storage device, or in other words redundant file elimination.

Archiving technologies leverage for all data within the environment. Data suited well for archiving technologies include:

- transactional databases (email, database applications)
- user files
- long-term file storage

Virtual tape library

Continuing to leverage backup software at the application layer of the server environment will most likely be required within your environment, although for some data backup can occur differently. In many environments, backup is written to hardware, although many advantages exist when writing backup data to a virtual tape library. A virtual tape library is often associated with the data de-duplication activity. A virtual tape library is easy to set up and can assist organizations to eventually eliminate the use of tape within their environments.

QRT – Using Technology for Business	
Summary of Systems and Components	A system is a collection of components. Most environments have multiple systems that frequently share components. A system streamlines technical and cyber operations, remediation and accountability using a persistent computing architecture.
Complexity of implementation	Many environments do not have an accurate inventory of their environment. Inventory of all components that are connected to any network is an important first step. Based on the inventory, you can begin grouping your components into manageable systems. Building from the manageable systems, you can begin to explore the level of persistent computing required to meet business objectives.
Starting fresh	Collect inventory prior to building the system. Include a lot of detail. Many applications are in the market to assist with this process. Understand your objectives, then plan out the technology that will be used.

Modifying existing environment	For existing environments, in most cases, validating existing inventory is the first step. The next step is to organize your "IT system" based on existing business processes and deliverables, for example email, database system, web services, and file storage.
Business Interruption	Minimal business interruption should occur.
Ballpark Pricing	Pricing is difficult for this subsection as it is very related to labor to collect and organize data and the deployment and type of persistent computing technologies that will be used.
Learning Curve	The learning curve is different based upon the technology leveraged. You must clearly understand your environment and map the technology that will meet the needs of the environment. This effort will minimize your cost and the impact of the learning curve.
FTE or Contractor	Defining the objectives for the organization is often executed by internal resources. The deployment and possibly the management of the persistent computing environment in the future may be FTE or contractor based.
Hints to get started	We've discussed several technologies related to persistent computing. Some example of questions and answers that may help as you review the needs for persistent computing within your environment. Take the following and create your own... Static and/or dynamic imaging: All solutions require the use of either static or dynamic imaging. • A node in an active/passive email cluster fails, how is the failed node rebuilt? In many environments the failed node is rebuilt manually, often forgetting small details. Static and/or dynamic imaging solves this problem, often for pennies on the dollar. • In the event of a hardware failure, can I quickly and consistently restore the hardware and or operating

system? Answer: yes, when using either static or dynamic imaging.

- In the event of contamination within the operating system and or software applications, can I rollback the hardware to a specific point in time without having to restore from a backup? Answer: yes, if using static imaging. Remember that static imaging is a point in time capture that is scheduled weekly, monthly, quarterly. There are several persistent computing technologies outside of basic imaging that can answer this question affirmatively as well.

- I need to have the service from a failed hardware available within the following time, 30 to 60 minutes or within four hours. Answer: persistent computing technologies can provide availability of a service within the time it takes to build server, although this question is focused on the recovery of the hardware once failed. If you need the hardware were stored within 30 to 60 minutes you will want to select dynamic imaging. It will take an estimated 30 to 60 minutes to restore the image (performance maybe faster on a higher speed network and system), although because you have selected a dynamic imaging you will not require time for updates and security patches.

- If you can wait for up to four hours for the restoration of the hardware, static imaging is a great solution. Static imaging will allow for you to rebuild the image within 30 to 60 minutes, dependent on the environment, although may require an additional 1 to 3 hours to update the image with patches and security updates.

Downloadable Tools	**Location:** https://goo.gl/joJuyf . **Filename:** SSP-A13-FedRAMP-Integrated-Inventory-Workbook-Template.xlsx 1- minute video on using the FedRAMP inventory collection tool (technical): https://youtu.be/WKeQaIGL3pk

Chapter 6: Cyber at the Core

Understanding the needs of your environment, your organization's strategic plan, and cybersecurity objectives is a good place to start when building your cyber strategy. A best practice is to evaluate the level of data protection required, using it as a "low" watermark to build upon. This is a good first step, although is a far stretch from understanding the cyber security standards your environment needs to be secure.

An alternative is to build your cyber security standards based on governing policies, or best practices, like the risk management framework or cyber security framework. The challenge for many is to align the standards and policies to the organizations cyber strategy and objectives. Perhaps use the keywords found in NIST 800-53, rev5 and match the key phrases to your organizations business needs.

The next step is to analyze compliance with the standards and policies you have established. I distribute those standards within my organization (to one or many sites) and I want to validate that the implementation language clearly demonstrates the sites understanding of that standard and will eventually lead them to compliance.

Step three is to protect the environment. So far in steps one and two we understand the security requirements, have built the security standards and policies, and implemented validation of our security standards and policies. In step three we are going to add accountability.

The implementation of accountability is dependent upon our ability to align real-time threat with our established security standards and policies. Absent of this alignment, we truly cannot have an accountable cyber environment

Cyber audits are a reality of life in the digital age. The question is how we can survive the scrutiny?

Let's start with highlighting a few key technologies that will assist any organization is preparing for an audit. Although the content of the book is very focused on cyber, the strategies and techniques apply to multiple business applications.

- Where do I begin enhancing my cyber posture?
- Many organizations know they should be secure, although where do they begin? And once you start, is it enough?

Step 1: Create a list of essential questions:
- How can I protect the data in my organization?
- I am not sure who is on my network, how can I monitor access to my environment?
- I have a lot of outside vendors like my air conditioning and building management, are they a threat?
- My IT person told me to purchase a firewall. Am I secure?
- And many others.

Step 2: Align questions to cybersecurity objectives:
- How can I protect the data in my organization? *Cybersecurity objective: Encryption*
- I am not sure who is on my network, how can I watch access to my environment? *Cybersecurity objective: Access Control*
- I have a lot of outside vendors like my air conditioning and building management, are they a threat? *Cybersecurity objective: Risk Management*
- My IT person told me to purchase a firewall. Am I secure? *Cybersecurity objective: Governance*

Step 3: Assign key phrases to cybersecurity objectives
Assign key phrases to each of the cybersecurity objectives and get started with you cyber strategy.

Selecting the right controls and policies

Now that we understand what our objectives are to enhance our cybersecurity policy, we need to find the correct controls and policies. Remember that we can use our key phrases to find the right controls, and the collection of those controls become our cybersecurity policies. *(There is an exception to this plan, and that is for those that are controlled by cyber regulations, legislation and laws. If your organization is bound to regulatory requirements, start with the controls defined within the regulation, implement those controls, then add additional controls to enhance your cybersecurity posture).*

figure 6 - Cyber Key Phrases

You may also want to try a free online service offered by BAP called bapOCS (Objective of Cyber Security). You can start with using bapOCS to build your policies, providing you with 100% flexibility related to the controls you add to your policy. bapOCS provides you with the opportunity to select from a group of cyber objectives to create the controls and policies needed for your environment. In addition to cyber objectives, you can create controls and policies based on regulatory requirements.

Sharing your cyber genius with others

Building a control allows you to define "what right looks like". A control provides an objective that can be monitored and consistent throughout the organization. There are multiple attributes when authoring a control that should be considered:

- Add weights to control allowing you to be specific as to the impact of variables that might threaten the effectiveness of the control.
- Group your controls into control bodies. The control body allows you to organize your controls, for example: Central office controls, NIST, ISO

- Add a brief description of the control objective whereas the control language is the detailed definition of the control objective.
- Take the time to associate key phrases with your controls, so that "like" purposed controls can be grouped and leveraged with in policies.
- Maintain your control objectives as the consistent and repeatable framework for all your security policies, while allowing the implementation language associated with the control to be very flexible to the multiple security policies within your environment. This will allow you to inherit, clone and efficiently update controls when they are leveraged in multiple policies within the environment.
- Create policies that are focused on an organization priority or business outcome. Generic, overarching policies are less than productive, and not a suggested best practice. With the inheritance of controls as your standardized framework, and in most environments inherited controls represent over 50% of the controls in any given policy, creating custom policies for business outcomes makes a lot of sense

Evaluate your current cyber tools?

The use of log aggregators and SIEM products have greatly enhanced our ability to find that needle in the haystack, allowing us to author scripts and algorithms to discover the threat to our environment and minimize the impact of a cyber audit. Over the course of time industries recognized great value in these products, although the effort required often exceeds that of the conventional IT administrator, and with the rapid influx of threat, additional tools are required to help us survive the audit.

Let's assume that we have 20 different components within our environment, remember a component defined hardware or software like network firewalls, operating systems, applications, and databases. Establishing a cyber strategy requires the implementation of cyber standards, often referred to as controls. The cyber standards include access to your system, encryption, insider threat, and a myriad of other cyber standards. For this example, let's assume there are 100 cyber standards.

With 20 different components and 100 standards, what is the impact of a single event to the controls? At any point in time can you declare the "cyber health" of an implemented control, if the answer is no, which often it is, perhaps ask yourself why? Understanding the impact of an event to the multiple components and controls is critical to understanding the actual health of the environment.

For example, the firewall is breached which had a direct impact on the access control standard, using 10 as high risk, let's assign a 9 to this breach. Because of the breached firewall, my LDAP server which typically a risk of 1, now has an elevated risk of 4. Remember there are 20 different components, although what are the total number of potential events per component?

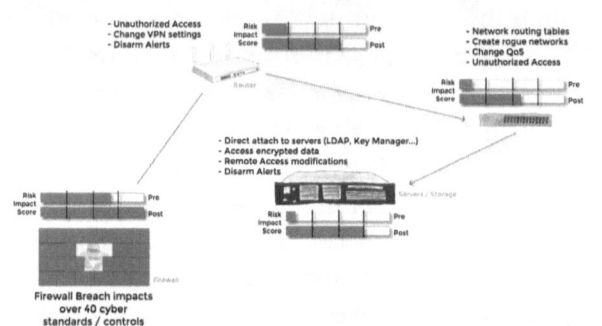

The router may have 5,000 possible events. We have only discussed the

figure 7 - Multi-layered impact

impact of a single event code and the relationship of that single event to components within our environment.

The use of SIEM or log aggregators can undoubtedly reduce the number of events to be processed, although the mathematical algorithms needed to understand the risk level impact is very complicated, based on the staggering potential implications and varying levels of impact. In a SIEM or log aggregator you would need to establish a set of weights and priorities assigned to each control and consistently calculate the variance to a declared level of risk.

Audit, compliance, and cybersecurity?

The time has come for all organizations to align with a cybersecurity baseline and begin the journey to accountability. I know for some organizations this may seem like an undaunting task, as frequently the requirements are issued by individuals that understand the cyber outcomes they desire, although may struggle to communicate the actionable requirements. A few examples:

- *GDPR:* If you are conducting business in the EU (Europe block) you will need to be compliant with GDPR, which is PII on steroids. GDPR is not a set of controls or policies, instead it is a legal document. You will need to establish the controls needed to be compliant with GDPR, and then extend the effort to enhancing your cyber posture for the organization. GDPR may start as compliance, although can easily be transformed into cybersecurity practices as well.
- *DFARS:* If you plan to perform work for the US DoD, DFARS should be top of mind. For the Civilian and Intelligence segments in the US Government... I am confident a DFARS like regulation is coming, so do not feel left out. DFARS as of January 2019 is a compliance activity, with self-certification and no direct fines.
- *23 NYCRR and CA A.B. 375:* If you are conducting business in New York, California and several other states you will fall under cyber/compliance laws with associated fines.

I have only mentioned a few of the security baselines; the list shares company with FISMA, FedRAMP, HIPAA, NERC, PII, PCI-DSS, GLBA, PHI, RMF, CSF and many others.

It is important to recognize there is a shift in the industry from "compliance" to "accountable security." Compliance does not always mean that you are secure and without risk. When developing your cyber strategy a few suggestions:

- You are not alone and do not have to start from ground zero. NIST, specifically NIST 800-53 provides the world's most complete set of security controls that will align with the security objectives of your organization. Use the NIST 800-53 controls as a starting point and modify for your environment.

Establish security controls that are scalable to multiple security policies. Build your new security controls based on existing controls  or NIST 800-53 controls and keep it simple.

Many of the new requirements have associated penalties for non-compliance. With established controls grouped into policy, you will have active proof of your efforts to maintain compliance, and a more secure environment. Your effort to become compliant should include a "roadmap" to continuous monitoring as well. Measure real-time threat to declare the integrity/effectiveness of the controls you have deployed.

Build and Discover your Cyber Needs

The challenge in the industry: do our efforts result in a compliant datacenter? Are we making it more difficult for cybercriminals?

A cyber policy is a foundational effort, the starting point for accountability within cyber operations. Without cyber controls and

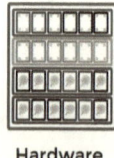
Hardware

Software

Process

Location

Cyber-Security Policy

figure 8 - Cyber Security Policy

policy, cyber defense is less than optimal. We may be able to defend against the known or predicted cyber threat, although, without stated objectives (cyber policy), organizations limit themselves to a flat dimensional view of the cyber threat. Establishing cyber policy is a starting point and has little to do with actual cyber protection. As we develop our cyber policy, we must include all the variables that may impact the "system".

Definitions

System: A system is the collection of hardware, software, location, people and processes that deliver a service to an organization. For example: all the hardware, software, operating system, the location of the data, the email administrators, the process by which a new email address is created... All of these and more would be considered the email system.

Hardware: All hardware associated with the system. This will include servers, storage, networks, firewalls, routers, etc...

Software: software includes applications, operating systems down to the "hidden" operating environments for the storage and network. All things software.

Process: processes include technical "cookbooks", standard operating procedures, troubleshooting procedures, etc. A process typically includes hardware, software, people and possibly the location.

Location: location can be a physical location or a virtual location like a cloud. The location usually defines where the hardware and software reside, not necessarily where the employees reside or the users of the system.

Cyber protection is in the execution and implementation of the cyber controls and policies, typically fulfilled by cyber operations.

As we continue to strive to enhance our cybersecurity posture, we must strike a balance between planning and execution. Too frequently a lack of balance between cyber planning and cyber operational activities can lead to risk in the environment. The key here is some security is better than no security. Building a cyber strategy is not a onetime event, it is a constant event as threat is very fluid, and modifications and improvement are continual.

The following "Cyber Steps" enable organizations to achieve Cyber Accountability.

Cyber Steps
Step 1: Build and discover your cyber needs
Step 2: Analyze and validate controls and policies
Step 3: Protect and provide continuous monitoring of your environment.

Start with a known and established collection of cybersecurity standards. The most significant collection of cyber controls is found within NIST, with the majority in Special Publication NIST 800-53. Regardless of your organization, the collection of standards within NIST are extensive and very impressive. Use the NIST control as a starting point and modify the controls to meet the requirements of your environment. Equally as important as building a collection of controls, is the management of the controls, the implementation language and the development of policy.

Save time and cost. When building your controls, use the correct tool. Preinstalled cyber controls and policies within the application.

The key to saving time and cost is to develop a set of controls that can be applied to multiple security policies. The objective of the cybersecurity control is a known variable, whereas the implementation of the security control will be modified based on the security policy. Providing consistency within the controls, which for many environments will be hundreds of controls, is essential for all systems (a collection of cyber controls to meet a specific business objective: e-mail, database, files) you wish to secure within your environment. Encryption, for example, is important to multiple systems within your organization, hence the encryption standard will be a constant, whereas the implementation of encryption will vary dependent upon the policy that requires encryption, for example: e-mail, file storage and web applications will implement encryption differently to meet the needs of their system. Some key attributes to building controls and policies:

- The ability to share cyber controls and policies with others using the same application, enabling a centralized site to create collections of controls and policies for other sites within their organization are key attributes of success. The ability to share controls and policies should be available for connected and disconnected environments and should always be free.
- The ability to inherit a single cyber control to multiple cyber policies. Inheritance should allow for a cascade effect when changes occur to your controls in the future, saving you time and cost.

Control framework

Following a successful discovery of cyber needs, organizations should have a framework to place all their controls and policies. Too often the hill to cyber accountability seems insurmountable, and we lose energy trying to complete all the controls and associated tasks, while the cyber threat continues to increase.

Security Controls / Standards

Security Baseline

"You have either been hacked or are being hacked and do not know it" FBI

figure 9 - Have you been hacked

What is Continuous Monitoring?

Continuous monitoring is often enabled through algorithms looking for known threat patterns, or the analysis of unexpected behavior within the environment. The understanding of threat to the environment is a step in the right direction, although the results must align with existing security standards to provide cyber accountability.

Cyber accountability is the ability to visualize the impact of the cyber threat to specific services or system (email, GOTs database, mission control) within the environment. Some of the attributes of cyber accountability include:

Automation and artificial intelligence to compare a standard to dynamic variables in an environment to ascertain the viability/health of the stated standard

Provide accountability, based on actual events, to the cyber health of an organization

Use of weights, priorities and key phrases to cumulatively ascertain risk level scores related to any standard and the impact on related standards to meet a common objective, cyber risk being a primary outcome

Focused resolution on non-compliant and risk-oriented events.

Continuous Monitoring and Accountable Security

Continuous monitoring is the first step; as is the deployment of SIEM, Log Aggregation, and Cyber Operations teams, although to understand the actual threat to the agency, the agency must move beyond SIEM and Log Aggregation into Accountable Cyber.

The use of log aggregators and SIEM products have significantly enhanced our ability to find that needle in the haystack, allowing us to create scripts and algorithms to discover the threat to our environment. Industry recognizes the value in these products, although the effort required, often exceeds that of the traditional IT administrator.

The impact of the firewall breach is not as simple as an exposed port on the firewall; the breach also increases the risk level of other hardware and software within the secured system. Because of the breached firewall, the risk level of multiple components increases, elevating the risk to the components within the AVSD system:

- The AVSD router risk score increased from a two to a seven
- The AVSD network switch risk score increased from a one to a four
- The AVSD LDAP server risk score increased from a two to a five

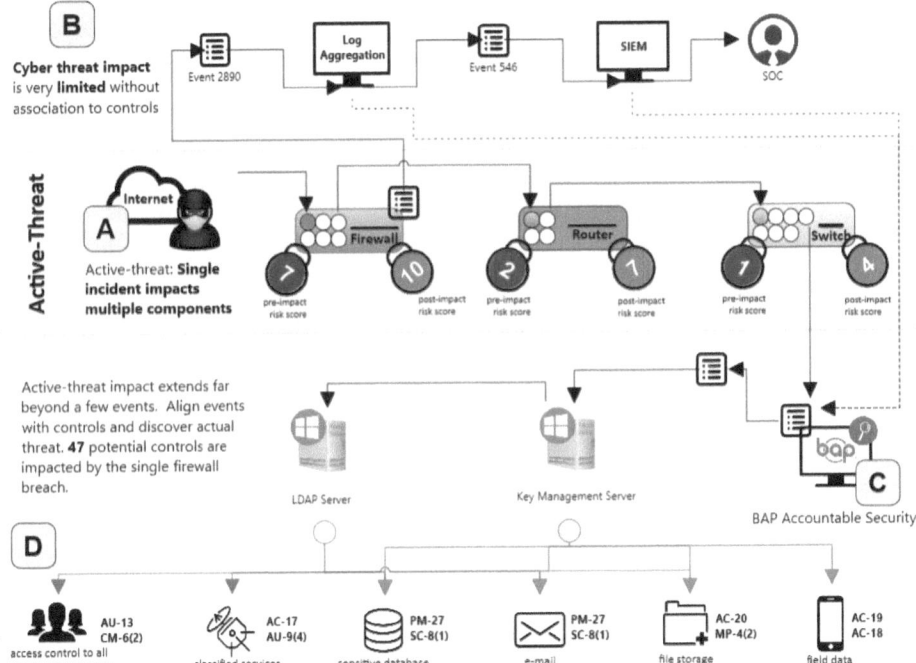

The use of SIEM or log aggregators will reduce the number of events to be processed, although the mathematical algorithms needed to understand the risk level impact is very complicated, based on the staggering potential implications and varying levels of impact, controls, and policies.

Organization accountability is possible

Achieving cybersecurity strength is possible when organizations view the creation of cyber controls and policies as the absolute point of reference from which we measure cyber accountability. Building an accountable cyber environment requires the correlation between active threat found in event logs to the controls and policies established within the environment and cyber strategy. The hardware and software manufacturers define the events, NIST and the local organizations define the cyber controls, both of which are known variables. As the event log produces a pre-defined and known error code, the event needs to be aligned with defined security controls, providing true cyber accountability.

Remediation – POA&M

As organizations identify and develop plans to address gaps in cyber analytic capabilities and risk management efforts. To address gaps organizations must first define a baseline that accurately captures their cyber objectives, for example, a cyber security framework / strategy. Then, draw a contrast between the actual state and the desired state of the controls, policies and baselines.

Prioritization of cyber health is dependent upon our ability to focus on systematic risks that begins with the discovery of events as they impact defined controls and policies. Events discovered within the environment should quickly prioritized.

Addressing the most significant risk first and focusing on the highest impact systems, assets and capabilities is a practical approach to cyber remediation. Remediation of risk is dependent upon understanding the direct and indirect impact of the cyber compromise.

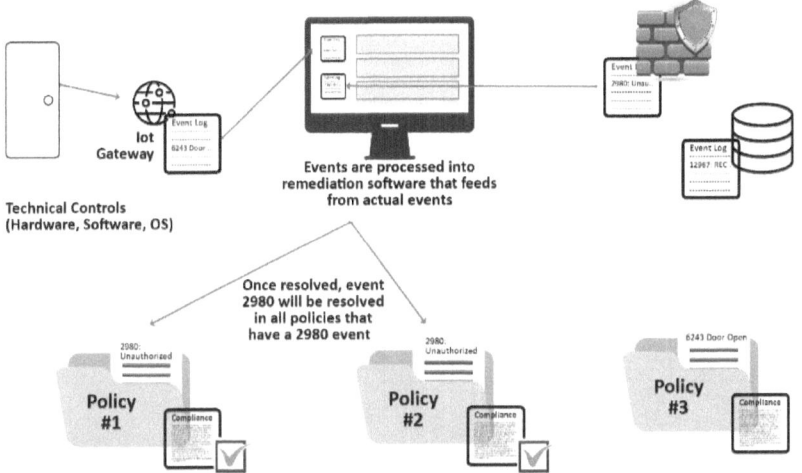

figure 10 - Remediation Steps

Once established, remediation efforts must be presented, organized and managed through the application of milestones, budgetary restrictions, third-party dependencies, assignment of resources and suspense dates. Align actual threat to the environment against established cyber controls and policies, funneling remediation requirements for immediate action.

Integration of remediation functions, within a control framework, enables organizations to identify and remediate risk quickly. As events are resolved, the event should be resolved for all associated remediation efforts. For example, event 2980 is resolved and updated for Policy #1 and Policy #2.

Security at the Hardware Layer

The x86 platform has several key security technologies that can be implemented to increase your security profile. In this section we will review several key technologies that have a direct impact on the server. Servers are core to our environment; hence improving the security of the servers will have a positive impact throughout the infrastructure.

Secure Boot

The boot cycle should include an encryption key found within the iLO silicon at the hardware factory. This highly secure encryption key approach, embedded in silicon, becomes the absolute point of truth for all server security operations. All other actions from the time of boot refer to this highly secure encryption key as the source of truth, making detection, recoverability, and cyber-security unmatched in the industry.

Embedded technology is no stranger to the highly secure environments like the US federal government. Some of the most secure systems in the world have been developed by the US government and reside on highly secure and specialized embedded silicon. The Silicon Root of Trust (SRoT) impacts multiple functional areas within an architecture, with direct and in-direct links to cyber health, a cyber baseline and security standards within the environment.

CAC 2 Factor Authentication

CAC-2 should be integrated into your server products, with the ability to revoke credentials as well. Recoverability from a compromise found either in firmware, the UEFI, or to a lesser degree, the operating system during the boot cycle and/or proactively during operation should be a default feature.

Secure Start

A silicon root of trust is a unique attribute that is unmatched in the industry which allows the boot process to perform a "secure start". As the servers are powered on, the iLO, found within the silicon root of trust validates and boots from its own firmware, then proceeds to validate the system BIOS.

This is an "absolute known secure state" as it is embedded within silicon. That means that every signature found within the silicon root of trust can be trusted and used as a secure baseline by which to measure/inspect all other components for tampering or compromise. If tampering or corruption is noticed, by default the iLO should alert the user and offer remediation steps or quarantine for forensic study.

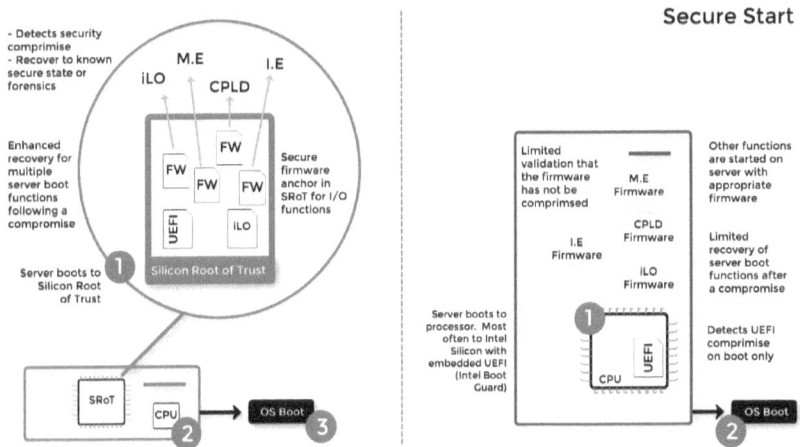

figure 11 - Secure Start

The "Secure Start" image illustrates two options for a secure start configuration, the option to the left, highlighted in green is the desired secure start configuration, although the option highlighted to the right in purple is typically found and represented as a secure start by many vendors. The key differentiator between these two options is the location of firmware actors within the environment. Notice on the left image the firmware is secured within the silicon root of trust, whereas on the right image, only the UEFI functionality is secured within he silicon. When selecting a server for your environment, always seek after the most secure server to enhance your security posture.

Secure Boot

Different then secure start, secure boot ensures that only firmware components, UEFI applications, and operating system boot loaders that have appropriate digital signatures, and are verified as authentic, can execute during the boot process, which can include third-party modules that had been digitally signed and validated as a set of trusted certificates embedded in the UEFI.

Because UEFI resides with in the silicon root of trust, it becomes very difficult, if possible, to compromise, as a result the trusted certificates of the third-party modules are very secure.

Many server manufacturers leverage UEFI, although with the UEFI in the highly secure silicon root of trust, customers can know that their certificates are very secure. If your security posture is built upon trusted certificates, which most environments are, it makes sense to ensure the certificates maintain their integrity and are not compromised.

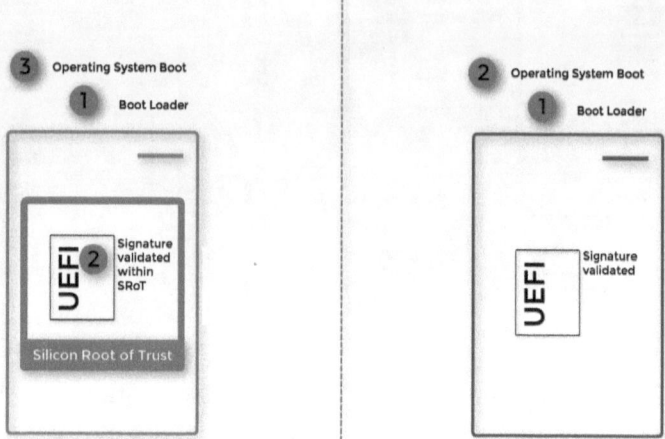

Based on the Secure Boot image, the left side, green, shows UEFI within the silicon root of trust which is a desired approach to securing the UEFI.

Dual Factor Firmware Signing

Dual factor authentication is certainly the standard when validating a user's access to a secure environment. The process and strength of dual factor authentication are rooted deeply in the military that use "challenge phrases" in combat zones. Firmware is very attractive to cyber criminals. It is the firmware within an automated/electronic system that governs and manages the activity of the hardware/software. Absolute security must accompany all interactions with the firmware, to include updating of the firmware. Many hardware manufacturers only update firmware that they have distributed, providing a good level of security. Although, unfortunately, the cyber threat today requires so much more. Armed with a silicon root of trust, firmware updates are subject to the rigor of dual factor authentication. When a firmware update is distributed, a desired state is to add an additional step to validate the firmware with the silicon root of trust. This allows the server to perform the first check of the firmware update as to the origin of the distribution, and a second check/dual factor authentication to the

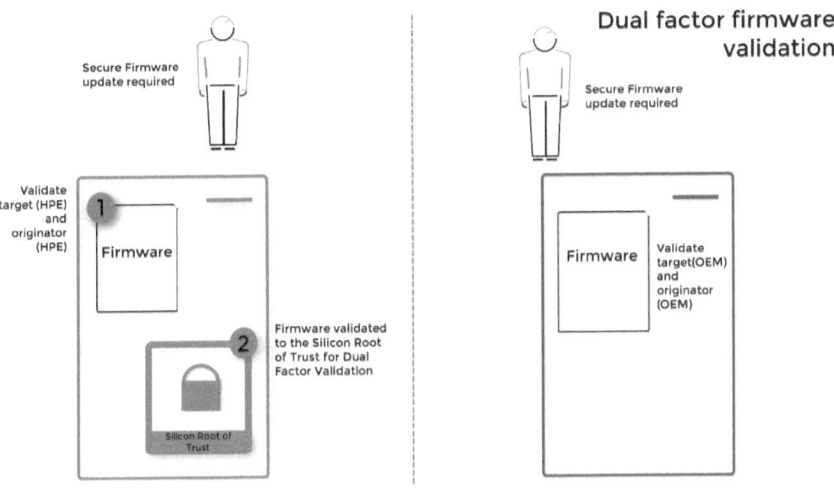

figure 13 - Dual factor firmware validation

highly secure silicon root of trust. An example can be found in HPE servers, as annotated in the "Dual factor firmware validation" image.

Residual NAND Data Erase

Firmware flash points are used to provide functionality to secure data storage within the sever. Several server OEMs can clean the data, although the desired approach is to erase all remnants of data on the drive, in addition, the ability to securely erase the NAND flash points as well, ultimately leaving no residual data on the server. This functionality will greatly enhance any organizations need to meet or exceed NIST 800-88 standards, as well as other security standards.

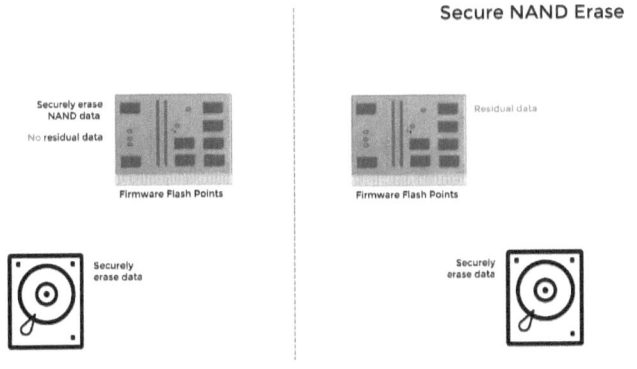

figure 14 - Secure Residual Data Erase

Automated Data Collection

Data collection activities, whether the organization forces regulatory requirements or performance objectives, information must be collected, managed, validated and ultimately become accountable. The information is obtained, which has a cost that includes data collection efforts/staff time, software to collect and organize the data, staff to review/manage the data - once, twice, three times before the information is submitted to meet the compliance need. The quality of the data and time required is a real cost to the organization that is realized in staff utilization and potential penalties as a result of the quality of the data collected.

Data collection activities extend deep within our organizations to include technical and non-technical efforts at an ever-increasing rate, making artificial intelligence and automation a must-have for all organizations.

Compliance is no longer a checkbox exercise. Regulatory compliance in 2018 continues to penalize organizations for noncompliance, with many organizations paying substantial fines and loss of business revenue. To exasperate the challenge, the cyber threat within our society continues to increase, making compliance activities a critical path to success for all organizations.

Building a data collection model

Building a data collection strategy typically requires little investment, merely a reallocation of resources. Many organizations continue to use a data collection strategy based on technologies and process dating back multiple decades.

With the increased data collection demand, now is the time to insert artificial intelligence to assist with your organization and move into the 21st century. Many organizations are making strides toward the future, although without simplified management, validation of our efforts, and continuous monitoring accountability, results are difficult to achieve.

1. *Simplify the creation and collection of data* through automated data collection all within a self-contained virtual appliance.

2. *Validation of information* provided by the individual submitting the data, as well as an enterprise view of all data collected.
3. *Continuous monitoring and accountability* of all information received ensuring the organizations best effort for continuous compliance, as well as non-technical reports for stakeholders to monitor their organization.

The collection and management of information both internally and externally is a difficult task, for most organizations there are 2 types of data collection:

- One time or reoccurring collection of information often referred to as "data calls".
- Regulatory collection required for compliance such as PII, PCI...

Efficiencies and cost savings are recognized as organizations leverage technology to assist with the process.

Common tasks for data collection

Multiple device collection. When information is distributed does the recipient have to use specific software to respond? The cost should be calculated for the software required. Convenience is an indirect cost based on the value of the data as it impacts additional cost or revenue streams within the organization.

Distribute/Collect/Manage information in a highly secure and network isolated environment. What is the value of information within sensitive areas?

Immediate User Feedback enables the recipient of the interview to be more accurate in their response, inadvertently lowering cost and increasing collection times.

Enterprise visibility of the data collected. The strength of the information collection is dependent on the ability to see all responses for the enterprise.

Correlate "real-time" events to the information collected, as applicable, continually providing the organization with continuous monitoring. With multiple regulations like GDPR, DFARS, PII and others, event correlation can be very powerful for organizations of all sizes.

1. Copy / Re-Use existing data collections. Solutions must provide the ability to copy, edit, delete, clone and use parts of past data collections.
2. Locate files. Ability to find data collections quickly in a structure environment.
3. Build custom data collections allows 100% flexibility as to the information collected.
4. Distribute data collections via social media, text message or email consistently.
5. Validate and re-certify the accuracy of the data collected, while providing feedback. For improvement. BAP software enables organizations to extend their current data collection leveraging technology to dramatically reduce cost and increase functionality within any environment, from business to the government.

To understand the cost of data collection and regulatory certification we need to assign time to each of the common tasks. Understanding this information allows us to get cost comparison to current labor intensive tasks within our organization.

Cost per data collection task	Labor hours for data call	Automated Used - Labor hours for data call
Correlate real-time events to collection	0	0
Copy / re-use data collected from the past	.5	.33
Locate files for the collection	.5	.08
Build custom data collections	4	.75
Validate collected information	10	.5
TOTAL LABOR HOURS	15	2.16

Based on a 72k annual employee salary performing the work, the cost for the data collection	$600	$86.67
Automation Used - Cost savings per data call		$513.33

Cost of certification

Cost per certification	Labor hours for certification	Automated Used – Labor hours for certification
Correlate real-time events to collection of certification information	80	.16
Copy / re-use data collected from the past certifications	1	.33
Locate files for the collection	.5	.08
Build custom data collections	8	.5
Validate collected information	125	8
TOTAL LABOR HOURS	214.5	9.08
Based on a 72k annual employee salary performing the work, the cost for the certification	$8,580	$363.33
Automation Used - Cost Savings per certification		$8,216.67

Your numbers may differ from the charts above. Perhaps ask yourself, if I send out a data call to 10 people, how much time will the effort require? We are very conservative and estimate that you will spend at least 15 hours.

Imagine sending multiple data calls, mix in a few certification and re-certification efforts, and you will soon discover the amazing time savings available when using automation. Time savings directly exposes cost savings, although the added functionality of automation will allow your organization to increase the accuracy and effectiveness of your data collection and certification efforts.

With an increased number of certifications and data collection efforts organizations struggle with effective management and accuracy of data collected. Work a little smarter without increasing the current budget. Consider the following:

1. *Multiple device collection.* When information is distributed does the recipient have to use specific software to respond? Convenience to answer your data collection will have a direct correlation with the success of your effort. Make is easier for the recipient and you will increase your data collection.

2. *Distribute/Collect/Manage* information should be consistent and intuitive. For annual certification image updating the information quickly over the course of the year. Do not spend time trying to remember where everything is located, use automation.

3. *Immediate User Feedback* enables the recipient of the interview to be more accurate in their response, inadvertently lowering cost and increasing collection times. Proving immediate feedback and suggested correction strengthens your data collection and compliance efforts, progressively getting better every year.

4. *Enterprise visibility* of the data collected. The strength of the information collection is dependent on the ability to see all responses for the enterprise. Enterprise management, distribution, comparisons, dashboards and

reporting should be the default for any data collection effort.

Validation

If the data collection has not been validated for accuracy, the data may create an increased workload that may cause the data to never be fully utilized.

As the recipient of the data collection request they complete their input and are provided with instant scoring of their content. Automation that leverages artificial intelligence uses a series of key phrases (customizable by the originator of the data collection request) and searches the provided content. If the key phrase is not found, the recipient is given hints and allowed to modify their submission. The result: The originator receives accurate input and the recipient receives training on expectations related to the data collection, a real win-win.

Validation scores are collected by all the data collection requests and forwarded to the enterprise for an enterprise view of the data collection.

Accountability

Beyond the validation of data collection, is continuous monitoring of the questions within the collected data that have electronic tracked events.

Often data collection and certification is a hybrid effort between technical and non-technical data. The line between data collection and certification and cyber accountability continues to blur.

Document ideas about your Strategy

www.ingramcontent.com/pod-product-compliance
Lightning Source LLC
Chambersburg PA
CBHW030846180526
45163CB00004B/1463